Cotton Denim DK

For Rosy Tucker and Penny Hill

Photography: Penny Wincer / Styling: Mia Pejcinovic / Pattern checking, editing and technical advice: Rosy Tucker / Book design: Sharlyne Slassi

Text and knitwear designs copyright © Debbie Bliss 2016. All rights reserved.

Contents

Basic Information

The quantities of yarn are based on average requirements and are therefore approximate. It is essential to work to the stated tension and you should always knit a tension square before starting. If you have too many stitches to 10cm/4in your tension is tight and you should change to a larger needle. If there are too few stitches, your tension is loose and you should change to a smaller needle. We cannot accept responsibility for the finished product if any yarn other than the one specified is used. Instructions given are for the first size, with larger sizes in round brackets. Where only one figure or instruction is given this applies to all sizes. Work all directions inside square brackets the number of times stated. See ball band for washing and pressing instructions.

Standard Abbreviations

alt = alternate
beg = beginning
cont = continue
dec = decrease
foll = following
inc = increase
k = knit
kfb = knit into front and back of st
m1 = make one st by picking up the loop lying between st just worked and next st and working into back of it
p = purl
pfb = purl into front and back of st

patt = pattern
psso = pass slipped st over
rem = remaining
rep = repeat
skpo = slip 1, knit 1, pass slipped stitch over
sl = slip
ssk = [sl 1 knitwise] twice, insert tip of left hand needle from left to right through front of both sts and k2tog
st(s) = stitch(es)
st st = stocking stitch
tbl = through back loop
tog = together
yf = yarn forward

yon = yarn over needle
yrn = yarn round needle
y2rn = yarn round needle twice to make 2 sts

USA Glossary

cast off = bind off
moss stitch = seed stitch
tension = gauge
stocking stitch = stockinette stitch
yarn forward, yarn over needle, or yarn round needle = yarn over

There will always be denim —

— and what could be better than a soft hand knit cotton produced in classic blues and sorbet pastels.

01

Cable and Lace Sweater

page 21

02

Diamond Lace Sweater

page 24

03

Cable and Basketweave Sweater

page 27

04

Tie Front Top

page 31

05

Military Jacket

page 35

06

Scoop Neck Sweater

page 40

07

Cabled Slipover

page 44

08

Tonal Cowl

page 47

09

Denim Jacket

page 48

10

Cropped Top

page 54

11

Denim Lace-Back Top

page 57

12

Cricket Sweater

page 60

13

Wrapover Waistcoat

page 64

01

Cable and Lace Sweater

To fit bust	81 – 86	92 – 97	102 – 107	112 – 117	cm
	32 – 34	36 – 38	40 – 42	44 – 46	in
Finished bust	116	128	140	152	cm
	45¾	50½	55	60	in
Length to shoulder	48	50	52	54	cm
	19	19¾	20½	21¼	in
Sleeve Length	37cm/14½in for all sizes				

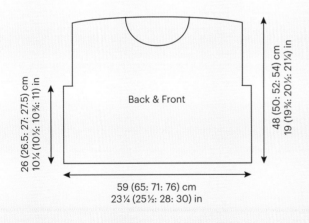

Back & Front

26 (26.5: 27: 27.5) cm
10¼ (10½: 10¾: 11) in

48 (50: 52: 54) cm
19 (19¾: 20½: 21¼) in

59 (65: 71: 76) cm
23¼ (25½: 28: 30) in

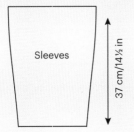

Sleeves

37 cm/14½ in

Materials

- 3(3:4:4) 100g balls of Debbie Bliss Cotton Denim DK in Pale Blue 05 (A) and four 100g balls in each of New Denim 02 (B), True Blue 03 (C) and Mid Blue 04 (D).
- Pair each of 3.25mm (US 3), 3.75mm (US 5) and 4mm (US 6) needles.

Tensions

22 sts and 28 rows over st st and 24 sts and 29 rows over patt, both to 10cm/4in square using 4mm (US 6) needles.

Abbreviations

See page 5.

Back

With 4mm (US 6) needles and B, cast on 141(155:169:183) sts.
K 1 row.
Now work in patt as follows:
1st row K1, [yf, k2, p3, p3tog, p3, k2, yf, k1] to end.
2nd row P4, [k7, p7] to last 11 sts, k7, p4.
3rd row K2, [yf, k2, p2, p3tog, p2, k2, yf, k3] to last 13 sts, yf, k2, p2, p3tog, p2, k2, yf, k2.
4th row P5, [k5, p9] to last 10 sts, k5, p5.
5th row K3, [yf, k2, p1, p3tog, p1, k2, yf, k5] to last 12 sts, yf, k2, p1, p3tog, p1, k2, yf, k3.
6th row P6, [k3, p11] to last 9 sts, k3, p6.
7th row K4, [yf, k2, p3tog, k2, yf, k7] to last 11 sts, yf, k2, p3tog, k2, yf, k4.
8th row P7, [k1, p13] to last 8 sts, k1, p7.
9th row P2tog, [p3, k2, yf, k1, yf, k2, p3, p3tog] to last 13 sts, p3, k2, yf, k1, yf, k2, p3, p2tog.
10th row K4, [p7, k7] to last 11 sts, p7, k4.
11th row P2tog, [p2, k2, yf, k3, yf, k2, p2, p3tog] to last 13 sts, p2, k2, yf, k3, yf, k2, p2, p2tog.
12th row K3, [p9, k5] to last 12 sts, p9, k3.
13th row P2tog, [p1, k2, yf, k5, yf, k2, p1, p3tog] to last 13 sts, p1, k2, yf, k5, yf, k2, p1, p2tog.
14th row K2, [p11, k3] to last 13 sts, p11, k2.
15th row P2tog, [k2, yf, k7, yf, k2, p3tog] to last 13 sts, k2, yf, k7, yf, k2, p2tog.
16th row K1, [p13, k1] to end.
These 16 rows **form** the patt and are repeated.
Patt a further 16 rows in B and 32 rows in C.
Cont in D only until work measures 26(26.5:27:27.5)cm/10¼(10½:10¾:11)in from cast on edge, ending with a wrong side row.
Shape armholes
Cast off 7 sts at beg of next 2 rows. 127(141:155:169) sts.
Work straight until 32 rows in total have been worked in D.
Change to A and cont until back measures 46(48:50:52)cm/18(19:19¾:20½)in from cast on edge, ending with a wrong side row.

Shape upper arms
Cast off 7 sts at beg of next 8 rows. 71(85:99:113) sts.
Shape shoulders
Cast off 11(16:21:26) sts at beg of foll 2 rows.
Leave rem 49(53:57:61) sts on a spare needle.

Front

Work as given for Back until front measures 38(40:42:44)cm/15(15¾:16½:17¼)in from cast on edge, ending with a wrong side row.
Shape neck
Next row Patt 51(56:61:66) sts, turn and work on these sts only for first side of neck, leave rem sts on a spare needle.
Dec one st at neck edge on next 12 rows. 39(44:49:54) sts.
Cont straight until front measures same as Back to upper arm, ending at armhole edge.
Shape upper arm
Cast off 7 sts at beg of next row and 3 foll right side rows.
Shape shoulder
Cast off rem 11(16:21:26) sts.
With right side facing, slip centre 25(29:33:37) sts onto a holder, rejoin yarn to rem sts, patt to end.
Dec one st at neck edge on next 12 rows. 39(44:49:54) sts.
Cont straight until front measures same as Back to upper arm, ending at armhole edge.
Shape upper arm
Cast off 7 sts at beg of next row and 3 foll wrong side rows.
Shape shoulder
Cast off rem 11(16:21:26) sts.

Sleeves

With 4mm (US 6) needles and B, cast on 57(57:71:71) sts.
K 1 row.
Work 16 rows in patt as given for Back.
Change to 3.75mm (US 5) needles and C.
1st and 3rd sizes only
Work 16 rows.

2nd and 4th sizes only

Inc and work into patt one st at each end of next row and 3 foll 4th rows.

Work 3 rows. 57(65:71:79) sts.

All sizes

Change to 4mm (US 6) needles and D.

Inc and work into patt, one st at each end of next row and 3 foll 4th rows.

Work 3 rows. 65(73:79:87) sts.

Change to A.

Inc and work into patt one st at each end of next row and 11 foll 4th rows.

89(97:103:111) sts.

Cont in patt until sleeve measures 37cm/14½in from cast on edge, ending with a wrong side row.

Place a marker at each end of last row.

Work a further 10 rows.

Cast off.

Neckband

Join right shoulder seam.

With right side facing, 3.25mm (US 3) needles and A, pick up and k30 sts down left front neck, k25(29:33:37) sts from centre front holder, pick up and k30 sts up right front neck, k49(53:57:61) sts from back holder. 134(142:150:158) sts.

1st rib row (wrong side) P2, [k2, p2] to end.

2nd rib row K2, [p2, k2] to end.

Rep the last 2 rows twice more.

Cast off in rib.

To Make Up

Join left shoulder and neckband. Sew sleeves into armholes easing to fit and with row-ends above markers sewn to sts cast off at underarm. Join side and sleeve seams.

02

Diamond Lace Sweater

To fit bust	81 – 86	92 – 97	102 – 107	112 – 117	cm
	32 – 34	36 – 38	40 – 42	44 – 46	in
Finished bust	111	121	131	141	cm
	43¾	47¾	51¾	55½	in
Length to shoulder	57	60	62	64	cm
	22½	23½	24½	25¼	in
Sleeve Length	45cm/17¾in for all sizes				

Materials

- 5(6:6:7) 100g balls of Debbie Bliss Cotton Denim DK in Banana 09.
- Pair each 3.75mm (US 5) and 4mm (US 6) knitting needles.

Tensions

22 sts and 28 rows over st st and 20 sts and 28 rows over patt, both to 10cm/4in square using 4mm (US 6) needles.

Abbreviations

sk2togpo = slip 1, k2tog, pass slipped st over.
Also see page 5.

Back

With 3.75mm (US 5) needles, cast on 110(122:130:142) sts.
1st rib row K2, [p2, k2] to end.

2nd rib row P2, [k2, p2] to end.
These 2 rows **form** the rib.
Work a further 10 rows and inc 3(1:3:1) sts evenly across last row.
113(123:133:143) sts.
Change to 4mm (US 6) needles.
1st row K2, [yf, skpo, k5, k2tog, yf, k1] to last st, k1.
2nd row and every wrong side row P to end.
3rd row K2, [k1, yf, skpo, k3, k2tog, yf, k2] to last st, k1.
5th row K2, [k2, yf, skpo, k1, k2tog, yf, k3] to last st, k1.
7th row K2, [k3, yf, sk2togpo, yf, k4] to last st, k1.
9th row K2, [k2, k2tog, yf, k1, yf, skpo, k3] to last st, k1.
11th row K2, [k1, k2tog, yf, k3, yf, skpo, k2] to last st, k1.
13th row K2, [k2tog, yf, k5, yf, skpo, k1] to last st, k1.
15th row K1, k2tog, [yf, k7, yf, sk2togpo] to last 10 sts, yf, k7, yf, skpo, k1.
16th row P to end.
These 16 rows **form** the patt and are repeated.
Cont in patt until back measures 55(57:59:61)cm/ 21¾(22½:23¼:24)in from cast on edge, ending with a wrong side row.

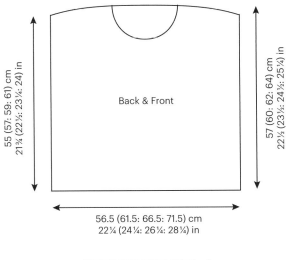

55 (57: 59: 61) cm
21¾ (22½: 23¼: 24) in

57 (60: 62: 64) cm
22½ (23½: 24½: 25¼) in

Back & Front

56.5 (61.5: 66.5: 71.5) cm
22¼ (24¼: 26¼: 28¼) in

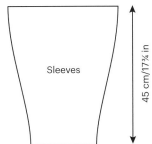

Sleeves

45 cm/17¾ in

Shape upper arms
Cast off 5 sts at beg of next 8 rows. 73(83:93:103) sts.
Shape shoulders
Cast off 8(10:12:14) sts at beg of next 4 rows.
Leave rem 41(43:45:47) sts on a holder.

Front

Work as given for Back until 22 rows fewer have been worked than on Back to upper arm shaping, ending with a wrong side row.
Shape front neck
Next row Patt 43(47:51:55), turn and work on these sts for first side of neck, leave rem sts on a spare needle.

Next row Patt to end.
Next row Patt to last 2 sts, work 2 tog.
Rep the last 2 rows 6 times more. 36(40:44:48) sts.
Work 7 rows, ending at side edge.
Shape upper arm
Cast off 5 sts at beg of next row and 3 foll right side rows. 16(20:24:28) sts.
Work 1 row.
Shape shoulder
Next row Cast off 8(10:12:14) sts, patt to end.
Work 1 row.
Cast off rem 8(10:12:14) sts.
With right side facing, slip centre 27(29:31:33) sts onto a holder, rejoin yarn to rem sts, patt to end.
Next row Patt to end.
Next row Work 2 tog, patt to end.
Rep the last 2 rows 6 times. 36(40:44:48) sts.
Work 8 rows, so ending at side edge.
Shape upper arm
Cast off 5 sts at beg of next row and 3 foll wrong side rows. 16(20:24:28) sts.
Work 1 row.
Shape shoulder
Next row Cast off 8(10:12:14) sts, patt to end.
Work 1 row.
Cast off rem 8(10:12:14) sts.

Sleeves

With 3.75mm (US 5) needles, cast on 42(42:46:46) sts.
1st rib row K2, [p2, k2] to end.
2nd rib row P2, [k2, p2] to end.
These 2 rows **form** the rib.
Rib a further 10 rows and inc 1(1:7:7) sts evenly across last row. 43(43:53:53) sts.
Change to 4mm (US 6) needles.
Work 6 rows in patt as given for Back.
Inc and work into patt, one st at each end of next row and every foll 6th row until there are 73(73:83:83) sts.
Cont straight until sleeve measures 45cm/17¾in from cast on edge, ending with a wrong side row.
Cast off.

Neckband

Join right shoulder seam.
With right side facing and 3.75mm (US 5) needles,
pick up and k29 sts down left front neck, k27(29:31:33)
sts from front neck holder, pick up and k29 sts up right
front neck, then k41(43:45:47) sts from back
neck holder. 126(130:134:138) sts.
1st rib row P2, [k2, p2] to end.
2nd row K2, [p2, k2] to end.
Rep the last 2 rows twice more then the first row again.
Cast off in rib.

To Make Up

Join left shoulder and neckband seam. With centre of
cast off edge of sleeve to shoulder, sew on sleeves.
Join side and sleeve seams.

03

Cable and Basketweave Sweater

To fit bust	81 – 86	92 – 97	102 – 107	cm
	32 – 34	36 – 38	40 – 42	in
Finished bust	96	107	118	cm
	37¾	42	46½	in
Length to shoulder	52	54	56	cm
	20½	21¼	22	in
Sleeve Length	46cm/18in for all sizes			

Materials

- 6(7:8) 100g balls of Debbie Bliss Denim DK in Pale Blue 05.
- Pair each of 3.25mm (US 3), 3.75mm (US 5) and 4mm (US 6) knitting needles.
- Cable needle.

Tension

22 sts and 28 rows to 10cm/4in square over st st using 4mm (US 6) needles.

Abbreviations

C4B = slip next 2 sts onto cable needle and hold at back of work, k2, then k2 from cable needle.
C4F = slip next 2 sts onto cable needle and hold to front of work, k2, then k2 from cable needle.
C3BP = slip next st onto cable needle and hold at back of work, k2, then p1 from cable needle.

C3FP = slip next 2 sts onto cable needle and hold to front of work, p1, then k2 from cable needle.
C4BP = slip next 2 sts onto cable needle and hold at back of work, k2, then p2 from cable needle.
C4FP = slip next 2 sts onto cable needle and hold to front of work, p2, then k2 sts from cable needle.
Tw2L = k into back of 2nd st on left hand needle, then k into the front of 1st st.
Tw2R = k2tog, then insert the right hand needle between the 2 sts knitted together and k1.
Also see page 5.

Panel A (worked over 12 sts)

1st, 3rd and 5th rows (right side) K4, p4, k4.
2nd, 4th and 6th rows P4, k4, p4.
7th row Tw2L, Tw2R, k4, Tw2L, Tw2R.
8th, 10th, 12th and 14th rows P4, k4, p4.
9th, 11th and 13th row K4, p4, k4.
15th row K4, Tw2L, Tw2R, k4.
16th row K4, p4, k4.
These 16 rows **form** Panel A and are repeated.

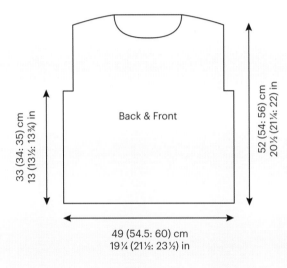

Back & Front

33 (34: 35) cm
13 (13½: 13¾) in

52 (54: 56) cm
20½ (21¼: 22) in

49 (54.5: 60) cm
19¼ (21½: 23½) in

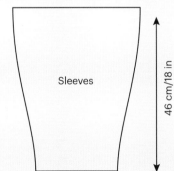

Sleeves

46 cm/18 in

Panel B (worked over 24 sts)

1st row (right side) P2, C4B, [p4, C4B] twice, p2.
2nd row K2, p4, [k4, p4] twice, k2.
3rd row P1, C3BP, [C4FP, C4BP] twice, C3FP, p1.
4th row K1, p2, k3, p4, k4, p4, k3, p2, k1.
5th row C3BP, p3, C4F, p4, C4F, p3, C3FP.
6th row P2, k4, [p4, k4] twice, p2.
7th row K2, p3, C3BP, C4FP, C4BP, C3FP, p3, k2.
8th row [P2, k3] twice, p4, [k3, p2] twice.
9th row [K2, p3] twice, C4B, [p3, k2] twice.
10th row As 8th row.

11th row K2, p3, C3FP, C4BP, C4FP, C3BP, p3, k2.
12th row As 6th row.
13th row C3FP, p3, C4F, p4, C4F, p3, C3BP.
14th row As 4th row.
15th row P1, C3FP, [C4BP, C4FP] twice, C3BP, p1.
16th row As 2nd row.
These 16 rows **form** Panel B and are repeated.

Panel C (worked over 24 sts)

1st to 6th rows [K4, p4] 3 times.
7th row [Tw2L, Tw2R, k4] 3 times.
8th to 14th rows [P4, k4] 3 times.
15th row [K4, Tw2L, Tw2R] 3 times.
16th row [K4, p4] 3 times.
These 16 rows **form** Panel C and are repeated.

Back

With 3.25mm (US 3) needles, cast on 134(146:158) sts.
1st rib row (right side) K2, [p2, k2] to end.
2nd rib row P2, [k2, p2] to end.
Rep the last 2 rows 5 times more, then the 1st rib row again.
Inc row (wrong side) Rib 56(62:68), m1, rib 22, m1, rib 56(62:68). 136(148:160) sts.
Change to 4mm (US 6) needles.
1st row (right side) P0(6:12), work 1st row of Panel A, p3, k4, p3, work 1st row of Panel B, p3, k4, p3, work 1st row of Panel C, p3, k4, p3, work 1st row of Panel B, p3, k4, p3, work 1st row of Panel A, p0(6:12).
2nd row K0(6:12), work 2nd row of Panel A, k3, p4, k3, work 2nd row of Panel B, k3, p4, k3, work 2nd row of Panel C, k3, p4, k3, work 2nd row of Panel B, k3, p4, k3, work 2nd row of Panel A, k0(6:12).
3rd row P0(6:12), work 3rd row of Panel A, p3, C4B, p3, work 3rd row of Panel B, p3, C4B, p3, work 3rd row of Panel C, p3, C4F, p3, work 3rd row of Panel B, p3, C4F, p3, work 3rd row of Panel A, p0(6:12).

4th row K0(6:12), work 4th row of Panel A, k3, p4, k3, work 4th row of Panel B, k3, p4, k3, work 4th row of Panel C, k3, p4, k3, work 4th row of Panel B, k3, p4, k3, work 4th row of Panel A, k0(6:12).

These 4 rows **set** the position of the patt panels, **form** 4-st cables between and are repeated.

Beg with the 5th row of patt panels, cont in patt working correct patt panel rows until back measures 33(34:35)cm/13(13½:13¾)in, ending with a wrong side row.

Shape armholes

Cast off 7 sts at beg of next 2 rows. 122(134:146) sts **.

Cont straight in patt until back measures 52(54:56) cm/20½(21¼:22)in from cast on edge, ending with a wrong side row.

Shape shoulders

Cast off 14(16:18) sts at beg of next 4 rows, then 12(13:14) sts at beg of foll 2 rows.

Cast off rem 42(44:46) sts.

Front

Work as given for Back to **.

Cont straight in patt until 16 rows fewer have been worked than on Back to start of shoulder shaping, so ending with a wrong side row.

Shape neck

Next row (right side) Patt 50(55:60), turn and work on these sts only for first side of neck shaping, leave rem sts on a holder.

Keeping patt correct, cast off 4 sts at beg (neck edge) of next row and 3 sts at beg of foll wrong side row.

Next row Patt to end.

Next row K2tog, patt to end.

Rep the last 2 rows twice more.

Next row Patt to end.

Work 5 rows in patt.

Shape shoulder

Next row (right side) Cast off 14(16:18) sts, patt to end.

Patt 1 row.

Rep the last 2 rows once more.

Cast off rem 12(13:14) sts.

With right side facing, rejoin yarn to rem sts on holder, cast off 22(24:26) sts, patt to end. 50(55:60) sts.

Patt one row.

Keeping patt correct, cast off 4 sts at beg (neck edge) of next row and 3 sts at beg of foll right side row.

Next row Patt to end.

Next row P2tog, patt to end.

Rep the last 2 rows twice more.

Next row Patt to end.

Work 5 rows in patt.

Shape shoulder

Next row (wrong side) Cast off 14(16:18) sts, patt to end.

Patt 1 row.

Rep the last 2 rows once more.

Cast off rem 12(13:14) sts.

Sleeves

With 3.25mm (US 3) needles, cast on 50(54:58) sts.

1st rib row (right side) K2, [p2, k2] to end.

2nd rib row P2, [k2, p2] to end.

Rep the last 2 rows 6 times more.

Change to 4mm (US 6) needles.

1st row (right side) P6(8:10), k4, p3, work 1st row of Panel C, p3, k4, p6(8:10).

2nd row K6(8:10), p4, k3, work 2nd row of Panel C, k3, p4, k6(8:10).

3rd row P6(8:10), C4B, p3, work 3rd row of Panel C, p3, C4F, p6(8:10).

4th row K6(8:10), p4, k3, work 4th row of Panel C, k3, p4, k6(8:10).

The last 4 rows **set** the position of the patt panel and **form** the 4-st cables at each side, with reverse st st at each end.

Beg with the 5th row of Panel C, cont in patt as set, working correct patt panel and cable rows, **at the same time**, inc and take all inc sts into reverse st st as follows:

Inc row (right side) P1, m1, patt to last st, m1, p1.

Patt 5 rows.

Rep the last 6 rows, 15 times more, then the inc row again. 84(88:92) sts.
Cont straight until sleeve measures 46cm/18cm from cast on edge, ending with a wrong side row.
Place a marker at each end of last row.
Work a further 8 rows.
Cast off all sts.

Neckband

Join right shoulder seam.
With 3.75mm (US 5) needles, pick up and k19 sts down left front neck, 22(24:26) sts from centre front, 19 sts up right front neck, then 42(44:46) sts from back neck. 102(106:110) sts.
1st rib row (wrong side) P2, [k2, p2] to end.
2nd rib row K2, [p2, k2] to end.
Rep the last 2 rows twice more and the 1st rib row again.
Cast off in rib.

To Make Up

Join left shoulder and neckband seam. Sew sleeves into armholes easing to fit and with row-ends above markers sewn to sts cast off at underarm. Join side and sleeve seams.

04

Tie Front Top

To fit bust	81	86	92	97	102	107	112	117	cm
	32	34	36	38	40	42	44	46	in
Finished bust	86	91	96	102	107	113	118	123	cm
	34	35¾	37¾	40	42	44½	46½	48½	in
Length to shoulder	35	36	37	38	39	40	41	42	cm
	13¾	14¼	14½	15	15¼	15¾	16¼	16½	in
Sleeve Length	30cm/12in for all sizes								

Materials

- 4(5:5:5:5:6:6:6) 100g balls of Debbie Bliss Cotton Denim DK in True Blue 03.
- Pair each of 3.25mm (US 3) and 4mm (US 6) knitting needles.
- 3.25mm (US 3) and 4mm (US 6) circular needles.

Tension

22 sts and 28 rows to 10cm/4in square over st st using 4mm (US 6) needles.

Abbreviations

sk2togpo = sl 1, k2tog, pass slipped st over; **ytb** = yarn to back; **ytf** = yarn to front.
Also see page 5.

Notes

* The fronts are knitted sideways from the side seams to the ties. They are given first so the back can be measured against the fronts and if your tension is not quite correct, the number of rows worked to the armhole and to the shoulder can be adjusted.
* When sewing side seams and shoulder seams, join approximately 3 sts to every 4 row-ends.

Left Front

With 4mm (US 6) needles, cast on 37(37:39:39:41:41:43:43) sts.
Shape side
1st row (right side) K14, ytf, sl 1, ytb, turn.
2nd, 4th and 6th rows Sl 1, p to end.
3rd row K22, ytf, sl 1, ytb, turn.
5th row K30, ytf, sl 1, ytb, turn.
Work 2(2:2:4:4:4:6:6) rows in st st across all sts.
Shape armhole
1st row Kfb, k to end.
2nd row P to last 2 sts, pfb, p1.
Cont in st st and inc in this way at armhole edge on next 4(6:6:8:8:10:10:12) rows.
43(45:47:49:51:53:55:57) sts.

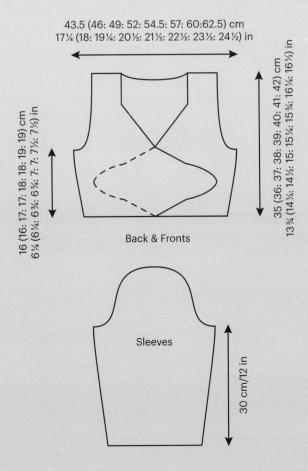

43.5 (46: 49: 52: 54.5: 57: 60:62.5) cm
17¼ (18: 19¼: 20½: 21½: 22½: 23½: 24½) in

35 (36: 37: 38: 39: 40: 41: 42) cm
13¾ (14¼: 14½: 15: 15¼: 15¾: 16¼: 16½) in

16 (16: 17: 17: 18: 18: 19: 19) cm
6¼ (6¼: 6¾: 6¾: 7: 7: 7½: 7½) in

Back & Fronts

Sleeves

30 cm/12 in

Next row (right side) Cast on 34(34:35:35:36:36:37:37) sts, k to end. 77(79:82:84:87:89:92:94) sts.
Beg with a p row, work 19(19:21:21:23:23:25:25) rows in st st for shoulder.

Shape neck
Cast off 21 sts at beg of next row.
56(58:61:63:66:68:71:73) sts.
P 1 row.
Dec row (right side) K1, sk2togpo, k to last 3 sts, k2tog, k1.
Cont in st st and dec 3 sts in this way on next 11(12:13:13:14:15:16:16) right side rows.

20(19:19:21:21:20:20:22) sts.
Next row P to end and dec 1(0:0:2:2:1:1:3) sts evenly across row. 19 sts.

Tie
** Work 12 rows straight.
Dec row K1, skpo, k to last 3 sts, k2tog, k1.
Work 7 rows.
Rep the last 8 rows once and the dec row again. 13 sts.
Work 5 rows.
Dec row K1, skpo, k to last 3 sts, k2tog, k1.
Rep the last 6 rows once. 9 sts.
Work 3 rows.
Dec row K1, skpo, k to last 3 sts, k2tog, k1. 7 sts.
P 1 row.
Dec row K1, skpo, k1, k2tog, k1. 5 sts.
P 1 row.
Next row K1, sk2togpo, k1. 3 sts.
Cast off **.

Right Front

With 4mm (US 6) needles, cast on 37(37:39:39:41:41:43:43) sts.

Shape side
1st row (right side) K to end.
2nd row P14, sl 1, ytb, turn.
3rd, 5th and 7th rows Sl1, ytb, k to end.
4th row P22, sl 1, ytb, turn.
6th row P30, sl 1, ytb, turn.
P 1(1:1:3:3:3:5:5) rows across all sts.

Shape armhole
1st row K to last 2 sts, kfb, k1.
2nd row Pfb, p to end.
Cont in st st and inc in this way at armhole edge on next 4(6:6:8:8:10:10:12) rows.
43(45:47:49:51:53:55:57) sts.
Next row K to end, turn and cast on 34(34:35:35:36:36:37:37) sts.
77(79:82:84:87:89:92:94) sts.
Beg with a p row, work 20(20:22:22:24:24:26:26) rows in st st for shoulder.

Shape neck

Cast off 21 sts at beg of next row.
56(58:61:63:66:68:71:73) sts.
P 1 row.
Dec row (right side) K1, skpo. k to last 4 sts, k3tog, k1.
Cont in st st and dec 3 sts in this way on
next 11(12:13:13:14:15:16:16) right side rows.
20(19:19:21:21:20:20:22) sts.
Next row P to end and dec 1(0:0:2:2:1:1:3) sts
evenly across row. 19 sts.
Tie
Work as given for Left Front from ** to **.

Back

With 3.25mm (US 3) needles cast on
84(90:96:102:108:114:120:126) sts.
K 3 rows.
Change to 4mm (US 6) needles.
Beg with a k row, cont in st st and work
6(6:8:8:10:10:12:12) rows.
Inc row K3, m1, k to last 3 sts, m1, k3.
Work 5 rows.
Rep the last 6 rows 4 times more and the inc row
again. 96(102:108:114:120:126:132:138) sts.
Work 9 rows.
Shape armholes
Cast off 7(7:7:8:8:8:9:9) sts at beg of next 2 rows.
82(88:94:98:104:110:114:120) sts.
Next row K2, skpo, k to last 4 sts, k2tog, k2.
Next row P to end.
Rep the last 2 rows 5(6:7:7:8:9:9:10) times more.
70(74:78:82:86:90:94:98) sts.
Cont in st st until armhole measures
19(20:20:21:21:22:22:23)cm/7½(8:8:8¼:8¼:8¾:8¾:9)in,
ending with a p row.
Shape shoulders
Cast off 7(8:8:9:9:10:10:11) sts at beg of next 2 rows.
Next 2 rows Cast off 8(8:9:9:10:10:11:11) sts, patt to end.
40(42:44:46:48:50:52:54) sts.
Change to 3.25mm (US 3) needles.

K 3 rows.
Cast off.

Sleeves

With 3.25mm (US 3) needles cast on
44(48:52:56:60:64:68:72) sts.
K 3 rows.
Change to 4mm (US 6) needles.
Beg with a k row, work in st st.
Work 6 rows.
Inc row K3, m1, k to last 3 sts, m1, k3.
Work 9 rows.
Rep the last 10 rows 6 times more and the inc row
again. 60(64:68:72:76:80:84:88) sts.
Cont straight until sleeve measures 30cm/12in from
cast on edge, ending with a p row.
Shape sleeve top
Cast off 7(7:7:8:8:8:9:9) sts at beg of next 2 rows.
46(50:54:56:60:64:66:70) sts.
Next row K2, skpo, k to last 4 sts, k2tog, k2.
Work 3 rows.
Rep the last 4 rows 4 times more.
36(40:44:46:50:54:56:60) sts.
Next row K2, skpo, k to last 4 sts, k2tog, k2.
Next row P to end.
Rep the last 2 rows 8(9:10:10:11:12:12:13) times more.
18(20:22:24:26:28:30:32) sts.
Cast off 3 sts at beg of next 2 rows.
Cast off rem sts.

Neck Edgings

Left front
With right side facing and 3.25mm (US 3) needles,
pick up and k77(80:83:86:89:92:95:99) sts from
shoulder to end of tie.
1st row Inc in first st, k to end.
2nd row K to end.
Rep the last 2 rows once more.
Cast off.

Right front

With right side facing and 3.25mm (US 3) needles, pick up and k80(83:86:89:92:95:99:102) sts from end of tie to shoulder.

1st row K to last 2 sts, inc in next st, k1.
2nd row K to end.
Rep the last 2 rows once more.
Cast off.

Lower Edgings

Left front

With right side facing and 3.25mm (US 3) needles, pick up and k80(83:86:89:92:95:99:102) sts from end of tie to side seam.

1st row K to last 2 sts, inc in next st, k1.
2nd row K to end.
Rep the last 2 rows once more.
Cast off.

Right front

With right side facing and 3.25mm (US 3) needles, pick up and k80(83:86:89:92:95:99:102) sts from side seam to end of tie.

1st row Inc in first st, k to end.
2nd row K to end.
Rep the last 2 rows once more.
Cast off.

To Make Up

Join shoulder seams. Join side seams. Join sleeve seams. Sew sleeves into armholes, easing to fit.

05

Military Jacket

To fit bust	86	92	97	cm
	34	36	38	in
Finished bust	94	100	105	cm
	37	39¼	41¼	in
Length to shoulder	52	53	54	cm
	20½	20¾	21¼	in

Sleeve Length (with cuff folded back)   44cm/17¼in for all sizes

Materials

- 6(7:7) 100g balls of Debbie Bliss Cotton Denim DK in Mid Blue 04.
- Pair of 4mm (US 6) knitting needles.
- 14 metal buttons and 7 flat buttons.

Tension

22 sts and 28 rows to 10cm/4in square over st st using 4mm (US 6) needles.

Abbreviations

pm = place marker; **sm** = slip marker.
Also see page 5.

Notes

The buttonholes are worked on the wrong side rows so they do not clash with panel shaping. Buttonholes are made in both fronts. The buttonholes on the right front fasten in the usual way.

The buttonholes on the left front fasten on the wrong side to flat buttons sewn behind decorative buttons on the right side.

Back

With 4mm (US 6) needles, cast on 89(96:101) sts.
1st row (right side) K1(0:0), [p1, k1 tbl] 14(16:17) times, k31(32:33), [k1 tbl, p1] 14(16:17) times, k1(0:0).
2nd row P1(0:0), [k1, p1 tbl] 14(16:17) times, k4, p23(24:25), k4, [p1 tbl, k1] 14(16:17) times, p1(0:0).
These 2 rows **form** a centre st st panel outlined with 4 sts in garter st and twisted rib to each side, and are repeated.
Patt a further 18 rows.
Next row (right side) K to end.
Next row P29(32:34), pm, k4, pm, p23(24:25), pm, k4, pm, p29(32:34).
The last 2 rows **form** a centre st st panel outlined with 4 sts in garter st which are marked.

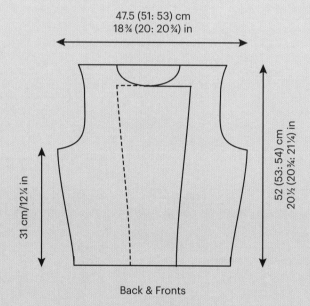

47.5 (51: 53) cm
18¾ (20: 20¾) in

31 cm/12¼ in

52 (53: 54) cm
20½ (20¾: 21¼) in

Back & Fronts

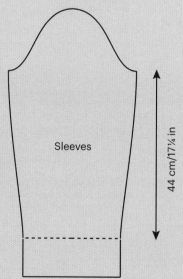

Sleeves

44 cm/17¼ in

Shape sides and centre panel

1st (inc) row (right side) K1, kfb, k to 3 sts before marker, skpo, k1, sm, k to marker, sm, kfb, k to 2 sts before marker, kfb, k1, sm, k to marker, sm, k1, k2tog, k to last 3 sts, kfb, k2. 91(98:103) sts.

2nd row and every foll wrong side row P to marker, sm, k4, sm, p to marker, sm, k4, sm, p to end.

3rd row K to end, slipping markers.

4th to 8th rows Rep 2nd and 3rd rows twice, then 2nd row once more.

Rep the last 8 rows 7 times more. 105(112:117) sts.

NOTE The 8 row patt will now be worked as follows, **at the same time,** shape armholes:

1st row K to 3 sts before marker, skpo, k1, sm, k to marker, sm, kfb, k to 2 sts before marker, kfb, k1, sm, k to marker, sm, k1, k2tog, k to end.

2nd to 8th rows will remain the same as before.

Shape armholes

Beg at 1st row of pattern as given above and keeping patt correct, cast off 5(6:6) sts at beg of next 2 rows. 95(100:105) sts.

Dec row K3, k2tog, patt to last 5 sts, slipping markers, skpo, k3.

Cont in patt and dec 1 st as set at each end of next 8 right side rows. 77(82:87) sts.

Patt 25 rows, ending with a wrong side row.

Inc row K2, kfb, k to last 4 sts, slipping markers, kfb, k3. 79(84:89) sts.

Work 3 more rows in patt.

Rep the last 4 rows twice more. 83(88:93) sts.

Work 2(4:6) rows more in patt.

Cast off.

Place markers at either side of centre 41(42:43) sts for back neck.

Left Front

With 4mm (US 6) needles, cast on 60(64:67) sts.

1st row (right side) K1(0:0), [p1, k1 tbl] 14(16:17) times, k31(32:33).

2nd row K4, p23(24:25), k4, [p1 tbl, k1] 14(16:17) times, p1(0:0).

These 2 rows **form** a centre st st panel outlined with 4 sts in garter st and with twisted rib to one side.

Cont in patt and work 3 rows.

1st buttonhole row (wrong side) K4, p2tog, yo, patt to end.

The rem 6 buttonholes are worked in this way on every foll 20th row (there will be no further mention of the buttonholes).

Work 14 rows in patt.

Next row (right side) K to end.

Next row K4, pm, p23(24:25), pm, k4, pm, p29(32:34).

The last 2 rows **form** st st with the centre panel outlined with 4 sts in garter st which are marked.

Shape sides and centre panel

1st (inc) row (right side) K1, kfb, k to 3 sts before marker, skpo, k1, sm, k to marker, sm, kfb, k to 2 sts before marker, kfb, k1, sm, k to end. 62(66:69) sts.

2nd row and every wrong side row K4, sm, p to marker, sm, k4, sm, p to end.

3rd row K to end, slipping markers.

4th to 8th rows Rep 2nd and 3rd rows twice, then 2nd row once more.

Rep the last 8 rows 7 times more. 76(80:83) sts.

NOTE The 8 row pattern will now be worked as follows, **at the same time,** shape armhole as follows:

Shape armhole

Next row (1st row of patt) Cast off 5(6:6) sts, k to 3 sts before marker, skpo, k1, sm, k to marker, sm, kfb, k to 2 sts before marker, kfb, k1, sm, k to marker, sm, k to end. 72(75:78) sts.

2nd to 8th rows remain the same as before.

Patt 1 row.

Dec row K3, k2tog, patt to end, slipping markers. 71(74:77) sts.

Cont in patt and dec 1 st at beg of next 8 right side rows and **at the same time,** inc 1 st as set on 6th row and foll 8th row. 65(68:71) sts.

Keeping armhole edge straight, patt 23 rows, **at the same time,** inc 1 st at set on 6th row and 2 foll 8th rows, ending with a wrong side row. 68(71:74) sts.

Shape neck

Next row Patt 23(25:27), turn and work on these sts only, leave rem 45(46:47) sts on a holder.

Patt 1 row.

1st row K2, kfb, patt to end to last 2 sts, skpo.

2nd row Patt to end.

3rd row Patt to last 2 sts, skpo.

4th row Patt to end.

Rep the last 4 rows once, then 1st row once more. 21(23:25) sts.

Patt a further 5(7:9) rows, ending with a right side row. Cast off.

Right Front

With 4mm (US 6) needles, cast on 60(64:67)sts.

1st row (right side) K31(32:33), [k1 tbl, p1] 14(16:17) times, k1(0:0).

2nd row P1(0:0) [k1, p1 tbl] 14(16:17) times, k4, p23(25:26), k4.

These 2 rows **form** a centre st st panel outlined with 4 sts in garter st and with twisted rib to one side.

Cont in patt and work 3 rows.

1st buttonhole row (wrong side) Patt to last 6 sts, p2tog, yo, k4.

The rem 6 buttonholes are worked in this way on every foll 18th row (there will be no further mention of buttonholes).

Work 14 rows in patt.

Next row (right side) K to end.

Next row P29(32:34), pm, k4, pm, p23(24:25), pm, k4.

The last 2 rows **form** a centre st st panel outlined with 4 sts in garter st which are marked.

Shape sides and centre panel

1st (inc) row (right side) K to marker, sm, k1, kfb, k to 2 sts before marker, kfb, k1, sm, k to marker, sm, k1, k2tog, k to last 2 sts, kfb, k1. 62(66:69) sts.

2nd row and every foll wrong side row P to marker, sm, k4, sm, p to marker, sm, k4.

3rd row K to end, slipping markers.

Rep rows 2 and 3, twice more and 2nd row again. 8 rows in total.

4th to 8th rows Rep 2nd and 3rd rows twice more, then 2nd row again.

Rep the last 8 rows 7 times more. 76(80:83) sts.

NOTE The 8 row pattern will now be worked as follows, **at the same time,** shape armholes:

1st row K to marker, sm, k1, kfb, k to 2 sts before marker, kfb, k1, sm, k to marker, sm, k1, k2tog, k to end. 77(81:84) sts.

2nd to 8th rows remain the same as before.

Shape armhole

Next row Cast off 5(6:6) sts, patt to end. 72(75:78) sts.

Dec row Patt to last 5 sts, slipping markers, skpo, k3. 71(74:77) sts.

Cont in patt and dec 1 st at end of next 8 right side rows and **at the same time,** inc 1 st as set on 6th row and foll 8th row. 65(68:71) sts.

Patt 23 rows and **at the same time,** inc 1 st at set on 6th row and 2 foll 8th rows, ending with a wrong side row. 68(71:74) sts.

Shape neck

Next row Patt 45(46:47) sts and leave these sts on a holder for neck, patt 23(25:27) sts, turn and cont on these sts.

Patt 1 row.

1st row K2tog, patt to end to last 4 sts, kfb, k3.

2nd row Patt to end.

3rd row K2tog, patt to end.

4th row Patt to end.

Rep the last 4 rows once more and 1st row again. 21(23:25) sts.

Work 5(7:9) more rows in patt, ending with a wrong side row.

Cast off.

Sleeves

With 4mm (US 6) needles, cast on 54(58:62) sts.

1st row [K1 tbl, p1] to end.

2nd row [P1 tbl, k1] to end.

These 2 rows **form** twisted rib.

Work 39 rows more in rib, so ending with a right side row of cuff.

Beg with a k row, work 8 rows in st st.

Inc row K1, kfb, k to last 3 sts, kfb, k2.

Work 9 rows in st st.

Rep the last 10 rows 8 times more. 72(76:80) sts.

Cont without shaping until sleeve measures 44cm/17¼in with cuff folded.

Shape top

Cast off 5(6:6) sts at beg of next 2 rows. 62(64:68) sts.

Dec row (right side) K1, k2tog, k to last 3 sts, skpo, k1.

Cont in st st and dec in this way at each end of next 8 right side rows. 44(46:50) sts.

Dec 1 st in same way as before at each end of 5 foll 4th rows. 34(36:40) sts.

Working decs on wrong side rows as follows: "P1, p2tog tbl, p to last 3 sts, p2tog, p1", dec 1 st at each end of next 10 rows. 14(16:20) sts.

Cast off.

Collar

Join both shoulder seams.

Edging

With right side facing and 4mm (US 6) needles, work across 45(46:47) sts on right front holder, pick up and k12(14:16) sts up right front neck, 37(39:41) sts from back neck, 12(14:16) sts down left front neck, work across 45(46:47) sts from left holder. 151(159:167) sts.

K 2 rows.

Next row Cast off 29(31:32) sts, k to last 29(31:32) sts, cast off. 93(97:103) sts.

Collar

With right side of garment facing, rejoin yarn to rem sts and K 1 row.

Now work in rib with garter st edges as follows:

1st row K4, [k1 tbl, p1] to last 5 sts, k1 tbl, k4.

2nd row K4, [p1 tbl, k1] to last 5 sts, p1 tbl, k4.

Work 1st and 2nd rows 9 times more and then 1st row once again.

K 4 rows.
Cast off.

To Make Up

Sew sleeves into armholes, easing to fit. Join side and
sleeve seams, reversing seams for turn-back cuffs.
Sew 7 metal buttons onto right side of left front to
fasten right front in the usual way. Sew 7 metal buttons
on right side of right front and 7 flat buttons behind
them on wrong side of right front, to fasten left front
underneath right front.

06

Scoop Neck Sweater

To fit bust	81 – 86		92 – 97		102 – 107		cm
	32 – 34		36 – 38		40 – 42		in
Finished bust	87		97		107		cm
	34¼		38		42		in
Length to shoulder	50		52		54		cm
	19½		20½		21¼		in
Sleeve Length	48cm/19in for all sizes						

Materials

- 6(6:7) 100g balls of Debbie Bliss Cotton Denim DK in Peach 07.
- Pair each 3.25mm (US 3) and 4mm (US 6) knitting needles.
- Cable needle.

Tension

22 sts and 28 rows to 10cm over st st using 4mm (US 6) needles.

Abbreviations

C2B = slip next st onto cable needle and hold at back of work, k1, then k1 from cable needle; **C4B** = slip next 2 sts onto cable needle and hold at back of work, k2, then k2 from cable needle; **C4F** = slip next 2 sts onto cable needle and hold to front of work, k2, then k2 from cable needle;

T4B = slip next 2 sts onto cable needle and hold at back of work, k2, then p2 from cable needle; **T4F** = slip next 2 sts onto cable needle and hold to front of work, p2, then k2 from cable needle.
Also see page 5.

Note

The finished bust measurements are approximate due to the nature of the cable patterns.

Pattern Panel (worked over 22 sts)

1st row (right side) P2, [k4, p4] twice, k4.
2nd row [P4, k4] twice, p4, k2.
3rd row P2, k4, p4, C4F, p4, k4.
4th row [P4, k4] twice, p4, k2.
5th row P2, [k4, p4] twice, k4.
6th row [P4, k4] twice, p4, k2.
7th row P2, k2, T4F, p2, k4, p2, T4B, k2.
8th row [P2, k2] twice, p4, [k2, p2] twice, k2.

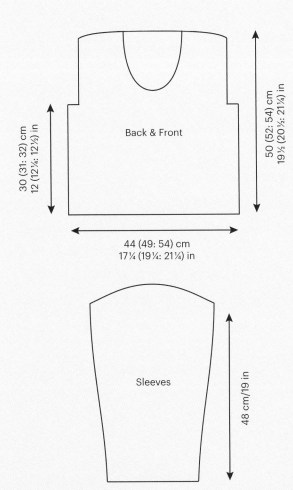

Back & Front

30 (31: 32) cm
12 (12¼: 12½) in

44 (49: 54) cm
17¼ (19¼: 21¼) in

50 (52: 54) cm
19½ (20½: 21¼) in

Sleeves

48 cm/19 in

9th row P2, C2B, p2, T4Г, C4Г, T4B, p2, C2B.
10th row P2, k4, p8, k4, p2, k2.
11th row P2, k2, p4, [C4B] twice, p4, k2.
12th row P2, k4, p8, k4, p2, k2.
13th row P2, C2B, p2, T4B, C4F, T4F, p2, C2B.
14th row [P2, k2] twice, p4, [k2, p2] twice, k2.
15th row P2, [k2, p2] twice, k4, [p2, k2] twice.
16th row [P4, k4] twice, p4, k2.
These 16 rows **form** the pattern and are
repeated throughout.

Back

With 3.25mm (US 3) needles, cast on 120(132:144) sts.
1st rib row P2(0:2), [k2, p2] 3(5:6) times, * k4, [p2, k2]
4 times, p2; rep from * 3 times more, k4, [p2, k2] 3(5:6)
times, p2(0:2).
2nd rib row K2(0:2), [p2, k2] 3(5:6) times, * p4, [k2, p2]
4 times, k2; rep from * 3 times more, p4, [k2, p2] 3(5:6)
times, k2(0:2).
3rd rib row P2(0:2), [k2, p2] 3(5:6) times, * C4F, [p2,
k2] 4 times, p2; rep from * 3 times more, C4F, [p2, k2]
3(5:6) times, p2(0:2).
4th rib row As 2nd rib row.
These 4 rows **form** the rib patt and are repeated
5 times more.
Change to 4mm (US 6) needles and work in patt
as follows:
1st row (right side) K0(2:0), [p2, k2] 1(2:4) times,
[work across 1st row of patt panel] 5 times, p2,
[k2, p2] 1(2:4) times, k0(2:0).
2nd row P0(2:0), [k2, p2] 1(2:4) times, k2, [work across
2nd row of patt panel] 5 times, [k2, p2] 1(2:4) times,
p0(2:0).
These 2 rows **set** the position of the patt panels with
rib to each side.
Cont in patt until back measures 30(31:32)cm/
12(12¼:12½)in from cast on edge, ending with a
wrong side row.
Shape armholes
Cast off 5(7:9) sts at beg of next 2 rows. 110(118:126) sts. **
Cont straight until back measures 48(50:52)cm/
19(19¾:20½)in from cast on edge, ending with
a wrong side row.
Shape upper arms
Cast off 6 sts at beg of next 6 rows. 74(82:90) sts.
Shape shoulders
Cast off 8(9:10) sts at beg of next 4 rows.
Leave rem 42(46:50) sts on a holder.

Front

Work as given for Back to **.

Cont in patt until front measures 33(35:37)cm/
13(13¾:14½)in from cast on edge, ending with
a wrong side row.

Shape front neck

Next row Patt 44(46:48), turn and work on these sts
only for first side of neck shaping, leave rem sts on
a spare needle.

Work 1 row.

Dec one st at end of next row and 9 foll right side rows.
34(36:38) sts.

Work straight until front matches Back to upper arm
shaping, ending at armhole edge.

Shape upper arm

Cast off 6 sts at beg of next row and 2 foll right side
rows. 16(18:20) sts.

Work 1 row.

Shape shoulder

Next row Cast off 8(9:10) sts, patt to end.

Work 1 row.

Cast off rem 8(9:10) sts.

With right side facing, slip centre 22(26:30) sts
onto a holder, rejoin yarn to rem sts, patt to end.

Work 1 row.

Dec one st at beg of next row and 9 foll right side rows.
34(36:38) sts.

Work straight until front matches same as Back to
upper arm shaping, ending at armhole edge.

Shape upper arm

Cast off 6 sts at beg of next row and 2 foll wrong
side rows. 16(18:20) sts.

Work 1 row.

Shape shoulder

Next row Cast off 8(9:10) sts, patt to end.

Work 1 row.

Cast off rem 8(9:10) sts.

Sleeves

With 3.25mm (US 3) needles, cast on 46(50:54) sts.

1st rib row P2(0:2), [k2, p2] 2(3:3) times, k4, [p2, k2]
4 times, p2, k4, [p2, k2] 2(3:3) times, p2(0:2).

2nd rib row K2(0:2), [p2, k2] 2(3:3) times, p4, [k2, p2]
4 times, k2, p4, [k2, p2] 2(3:3) times, k2(0:2).

3rd rib row P2(0:2), [k2, p2] 2(3:3) times, C4F, [p2, k2]
4 times, p2, C4F, [k2, p2] 2(3:3) times, p2(0:2).

4th rib row As 2nd rib row.

These 4 rows **form** the rib patt and are repeated
5 times more.

Change to 4mm (US 6) needles and work in patt
as follows:

1st row (right side) P0(0:2), k0(2:2), [work across 1st
row of patt panel] twice, p2, k0(2:2), p0(0:2).

2nd row K0(0:2), p0(2:2), k2, [work across 1st row of
patt panel] twice, p0(2:2), k0(0:2).

These 2 rows **set** the position of the patt panels with
rib to each side.

Working correct patt panel rows, inc one st at each
end of the next row and every foll 6th row until there
are 80(84:88) sts, working extra sts into k2, p2 rib.

Work straight until sleeve measures 48cm/19in from
cast on edge, ending with a wrong side row.

Place a marker at each end of last row.

Work a further 6(8:10) rows.

Shape sleeve top

Cast off 3 sts at beg of next 18 rows. 26(30:34) sts.

Cast off.

Neckband

Join right shoulder seam.

With right side facing and 3.25mm (US 3) needles, pick
up and k33 sts down left side of front neck, k22(26:30)
sts from front neck holder, pick up and k33 sts up
right side of front neck, k42(46:50) sts from back neck
holder. 130(138:146) sts.

1st rib row P2, [k2, p2] to end.

2nd row K2, [p2, k2] to end.

Rep the last 2 rows twice more and the first row again.
Cast off in rib.

To Make Up

Join left shoulder and neckband seam. Sew sleeves
into armholes, with row-ends above markers sewn to
sts cast off at beg of armhole shaping.
Join side and sleeve seams.

07

Cabled Slipover

To fit bust	81	86	92	97	102	107	112	cm
	32	34	36	38	40	42	44	in
Finished bust	86	92	98	104	110	116	122	cm
	34	36	38½	41	43¼	45½	48	in
Length to shoulder	48	49	50	51	52	54	56	cm
	19	19¼	19¾	20	20½	21¼	22	in

Back & Front

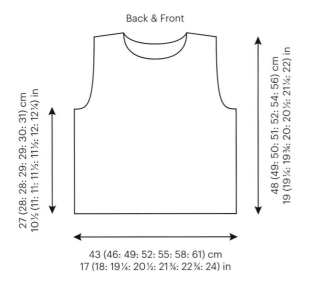

27 (28: 28: 29: 29: 30: 31) cm
10½ (11: 11: 11½: 11½: 12: 12¼) in

48 (49: 50: 51: 52: 54: 56) cm
19 (19¼: 19¾: 20: 20½: 21¼: 22) in

43 (46: 49: 52: 55: 58: 61) cm
17 (18: 19¼: 20½: 21¾: 22¾: 24) in

Materials

- 4(4:5:5:5:6:6) 100g balls of Debbie Bliss Cotton Denim DK in Mint 08.
- Pair each 3.25 (US 3) and 4mm (US 6) knitting needles.
- Cable needle.

Tension

24 sts and 32 rows to 10cm/4in square over st st using 4mm (US 6) needles.

Abbreviations

C4B = slip next 2 sts onto cable needle and hold at back of work, k2, then k2 from cable needle; **C4F** = slip next 2 sts onto cable needle and hold at front of work, k2, then k2 from cable needle; **T3B** = slip next st onto cable needle and hold at back of work, k2, then p1 from cable needle; **T3F** = slip next 2 sts onto cable needle and hold to front of work, p1, then k2 from cable needle; **T4B** = slip next 2 sts onto cable needle and hold at back of work, k2, then p2 from cable needle; **T4F** = slip next 2 sts onto cable needle and hold to front of work, p2, then k2 from cable needle; **Tw2R** = k into 2nd st on left hand needle, then k into first st and slip both sts off together.
Also see page 5.

Pattern Panel (worked over 24 sts)
1st row (right side) P2, C4B, [p4, C4B] twice, p2.
2nd row K2, p4, [k4, p4] twice, k2.
3rd row P1, T3B, [T4F, T4B] twice, T3F, p1.
4th row K1, p2, k3, p4, k4, p4, k3, p2, k1.
5th row T3B, p3, C4F, p4, C4F, p3, T3F.
6th row P2, k4, [p4, k4] twice, p2.
7th row K2, p3, T3B, T4F, T4B, T3F, p3, k2.
8th row [P2, k3] twice, p4, [k3, p2] twice.
9th row [K2, p3] twice, C4B, [p3, k2] twice.
10th row As 8th row.
11th row K2, p3, T3F, T4B, T4F, T3B, p3, k2.
12th row As 6th row.
13th row T3F, p3, C4F, p4, C4F, p3, T3B.
14th row As 4th row.
15th row P1, T3F, [T4B, T4F] twice, T3B, p1.
16th row As 2nd row.
These 16 rows **form** the patt and are repeated throughout.

Back

With 3.25mm (US 3) needles, cast on
124(132:140:148:156:164:172) sts.
1st rib row (right side) [P2, k2] 12(13:14:15:16:17:18)
times, p4, [k4, p4] 3 times, [k2, p2] 12(13:14:15:16:17:18)
times.
2nd rib row [K2, p2] 12(13:14:15:16:17:18) times, k4, [p4,
k4] 3 times, [p2, k2] 12(13:14:15:16:17:18) times.
3rd rib row [P2, Tw2R] 6(7:8:9:10:11:12) times, * [p2, k2]
twice, p2, Tw2R; rep from * once more, p4, [k4, p4]
3 times, ** Tw2R, p2, [k2, p2] twice; rep from ** once
more, [Tw2R, p2] 6(7:8:9:10:11:12) times.
Rep the last 2 rows until rib measures 10cm/4in from
cast on edge, ending with a 3rd rib row.
Inc row (wrong side) [K2, p2] 6(7:8:9:10:11:12) times,
* k2, p2, k2, m1, p2, m1, k2, p2; rep from * once more,
k4, [p4, k4] 3 times, ** p2, k2, m1, p2, m1, k2, p2, k2;
rep from ** once more, [p2, k2] 6(7:8:9:10:11:12) times.
132(140:148:156:164:172:180) sts.
Change to 4mm (US 6) needles.

1st row [P2, Tw2R] 6(7:8:9:10:11:12) times, * p2, k8, p2,
Tw2R; rep from * once more, p2, work across 1st row
of patt panel, p2, ** Tw2R, p2, k8, p2; rep from ** once
more, [Tw2R, p2] 6(7:8:9:10:11:12) times.
2nd row [K2, p2] 6(7:8:9:10:11:12) times, * k2, p8, k2,
p2; rep from * once more, k2, work across 2nd row of
patt panel, k2, ** p2, k2, p8, k2; rep from ** once more,
[p2, k2] 6(7:8:9:10:11:12) times.
3rd row [P2, Tw2R] 6(7:8:9:10:11:12) times, * p2, C4B,
C4F, p2, Tw2R; rep from * once more, p2, work across
3rd row of patt panel, p2, ** Tw2R, p2, C4B, C4F, p2;
rep from ** once more, [Tw2R, p2] 6(7:8:9:10:11:12) times.
4th row [K2, p2] 6(7:8:9:10:11:12) times, * k2, p8, k2, p2;
rep from * once more, k2, work across 4th row of patt
panel, k2, ** p2, k2, p8, k2; rep from ** once more, [p2,
k2] 6(7:8:9:10:11:12) times.
These 4 rows **set** the position for the patt panel and
form the 8-st cable panel.
Cont in patt working correct patt rows until back
measures 27(28:28:29:29:30:31)cm/10½(11:11:11½:
11½:12:12¼)in from cast on edge, ending with a wrong
side row.
Shape armholes
Cast off 10(11:12:13:14:15:16) sts at beg of next 2 rows.
112(118:124:130:136:142:148) sts.
Dec one st at each end of next row and 6(7:8:9:10:11:12)
foll right side rows. 98(102:106:110:114:118:122) sts. **
Cont straight in patt until back measures
44(45:46:47:48:50:52)cm/17¼(17¾:18:18½:19:19¾:20½)
in from cast on edge, ending with a wrong side row.
Shape neck
Next row Patt 35(37:39:41:43:45:47), turn and work on
these sts only for first side of neck shaping, leave rem
sts on a spare needle.
Dec one st at neck edge on next 8 rows.
27(29:31:33:35:37:39) sts.
Work 5 rows.
Shape shoulder
Cast off 13(14:15:16:17:18:19) sts at beg of next row.
Work 1 row.
Cast off rem 14(15:16:17:18:19:20) sts.

With right side facing, slip centre 28 sts onto a holder, rejoin yarn to rem sts on spare needle, patt to end.
Dec one st at neck edge on next 8 rows.
27(29:31:33:35:37:39) sts.
Work 6 rows.

Shape shoulder
Cast off 13(14:15:16:17:18:19) sts at beg of next row.
Work 1 row.
Cast off rem 14(15:16:17:18:19:20) sts.

Front

Work as given for Back to **.
Cont straight in patt until front measures 39(40:41:42:43:44:45)cm/15¼(15¾:16¼:16½:17:17¼:17¾) in from cast on edge, ending with a wrong side row.

Shape neck
Next row Patt 39(41:43:45:47:49:51), turn and work on these sts only for first side of neck shaping, leave rem sts on a spare needle.
Dec one st at neck edge on next 12 rows.
27(29:31:33:35:37:39) sts.
Work straight until front matches Back to shoulder shaping ending at armhole edge.

Shape shoulder
Cast off 13(14:15:16:17:18:19) sts at beg of next row.
Work 1 row.
Cast off rem 14(15:16:17:18:19:20) sts.
With right side facing, slip centre 20 sts onto a holder, rejoin yarn to rem sts on spare needle, patt to end.
Dec one st at neck edge on next 12 rows.
27(29:31:33:35:37:39) sts.
Work straight until front matches Back to shoulder shaping ending at armhole edge.

Shape shoulder
Cast off 13(14:15:16:17:18:19) sts at beg of next row.
Work 1 row.
Cast off rem 14(15:16:17:18:19:20) sts.

Neckband

Join right shoulder seam.
With right side facing and 3.25mm (US 3) needles, pick up and k24 sts down left front neck, k across 20 sts at centre front, pick up and k24 sts up right front neck, 11 sts down right back neck, k across 28 sts at back neck, pick up and k11 sts up left back neck.
118 sts.
1st rib row P2, [k2, p2] to end.
2nd rib row K2, [p2, k2] to end.
Rep the last 2 rows once more and the 1st row again.
Cast off in rib.

Armbands

Join left shoulder and neckband seam.
With right side facing and 3.25mm (US 3) needles, pick up and k122(126:126:130:130:134:138) sts evenly around armhole edge.
Work 5 rows in rib as given for Neckband.
Cast off in rib.

To Make Up

Join side and armband seams.

08

Tonal Cowl

Size One size approximately 18cm/7in deep x 120cm/47in circumference.

Materials
- One 100g ball in each of Debbie Bliss Cotton Denim DK in each of New Denim 02 (A), True Blue 03 (B) and Mid Blue 04 (C) (see Note).
- Pair of 4mm (US 6) needles.

Tensions
22 sts and 28 rows over st st and 24 sts and 29 rows over patt, both to 10cm/4in square using 4mm (US 6) needles.

Abbreviations
See page 5.

Note
You will need approximately 50g of each colour.

Back and Front (both alike)

With 4mm (US 6) needles and A, cast on 141 sts.
K 1 row.
Work in patt as follows:
1st row (right side) K1, [yf, k2, p3, p3tog, p3, k2, yf, k1] to end.
2nd row P4, [k7, p7] to last 11 sts, k7, p4.
3rd row K2, [yf, k2, p2, p3tog, p2, k2, yf, k3] to last 13 sts, yf, k2, p2, p3tog, p2, k2, yf, k2.
4th row P5, [k5, p9] to last 10 sts, k5, p5.

5th row K3, [yf, k2, p1, p3tog, p1, k2, yf, k5] to last 12 sts, yf, k2, p1, p3tog, p1, k2, yf, k3.
6th row P6, [k3, p11] to last 9 sts, k3, p6.
7th row K4, [yf, k2, p3tog, k2, yf, k7] to last 11 sts, yf, k2, p3tog, k2, yf, k4.
8th row P7, [k1, p13] to last 8 sts, k1, p7.
9th row P2tog, [p3, k2, yf, k1, yf, k2, p3, p3tog] to last 13 sts, p3, k2, yf, k1, yf, k2, p3, p2tog.
10th row K4, [p7, k7] to last 11 sts, p7, k4.
11th row P2tog, [p2, k2, yf, k3, yf, k2, p2, p3tog] to last 13 sts, p2, k2, yf, k3, yf, k2, p2, p2tog.
12th row K3, [p9, k5] to last 12 sts, p9, k3.
13th row P2tog, [p1, k2, yf, k5, yf, k2, p1, p3tog] to last 13 sts, p1, k2, yf, k5, yf, k2, p1, p2tog.
14th row K2, [p11, k3] to last 13 sts, p11, k2.
15th row P2tog, [k2, yf, k7, yf, k2, p3tog] to last 13 sts, k2, yf, k7, yf, k2, p2tog.
16th row K1, [p13, k1] to end.
These 16 rows **form** the patt and are repeated.
Patt a further 16 rows in B, then 14 rows in C.
Next row P2tog, [k11, p3tog] to last 13 sts, k11, p2tog.
130 sts.
Cast off knitwise on wrong side.

To Make Up
Join row-end seam.

09

Denim Jacket

	81 – 86		92 – 97		102 – 107	
To fit bust	81 – 86		92 – 97		102 – 107	cm
	32 – 34		36 – 38		40 – 42	in
Finished bust	94		104		114	cm
	37		41		45	in
Length to shoulder	49		50		51	cm
	19¼		19¾		20	in
Sleeve Length	45		46		48	cm
	17¾		18		19	in

Materials

- 6(7:8) 100g balls of Debbie Bliss Cotton Denim DK in Charcoal 01.
- Pair each of 3.75mm (US 5) and 4mm (US 6) knitting needles.
- Cable needle.
- 9 small buttons.

Tension

22 sts and 28 rows to 10cm/4in square over st st using 4mm (US 6) needles.

Abbreviations

C4B = slip next 2 sts onto cable needle and hold at back of work, k2, then k2 from cable needle;
C4F = slip next 2 sts onto cable needle and hold to front of work, k2, then k2 from cable needle.
Also see page 5.

Patt Panel A (worked over 6 sts)

1st row (wrong side) K1, p4, k1.
2nd row P1, C4B, p1.
3rd row K1, p4, k1.
4th row P1, k4, p1.
These 4 rows **form** panel A and are repeated.

Patt Panel B (worked over 6 sts)

Work as Cable A, but on 2nd row, work C4F in place of C4B.

Patt Panel C (worked over 17 sts)

1st row (wrong side) K1, p4, k2, p1, k1, p1, k2, p4, k1.
2nd row P1, C4B, p1, [k1, p1] 3 times, C4F, p1.
3rd row As 1st row.
4th row P1, k4, p1, [k1, p1] 3 times, k4, p1.
These 4 rows **form** panel C and are repeated.

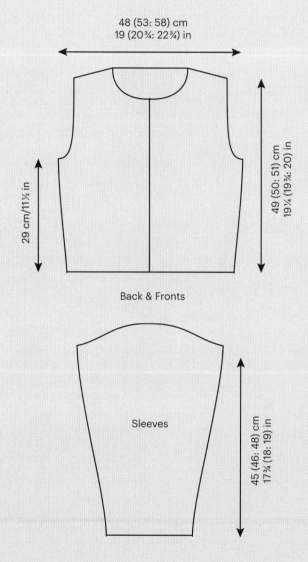

48 (53: 58) cm
19 (20¾: 22¾) in

49 (50: 51) cm
19¼ (19¾: 20) in

29 cm/11½ in

Back & Fronts

45 (46: 48) cm
17¾ (18: 19) in

Sleeves

Back

With 3.75mm (US 5) needles, cast on 101(113:125) sts.

Moss st row K1, [p1, k1] to end.

Rep this row 7 times more.

Inc row (right side) K15(19:23), p1, k2, m1, k1, p1, k15, p1, k2, m1, k1, p1, k3(5:7), p1, k2, m1, k1, p1, k1, [p1, k1] twice, p1, k2, m1, k1, p1, k3(5:7), p1, k2, m1, k1, p1, k15, p1, k2, m1, k1, p1, k15(19:23). 107(119:131) sts.

Change to 4mm (US 6) needles.

1st row (wrong side) P15(19:23), work 1st row patt A, p15, work 1st row patt A, p3(5:7), work 1st row patt C, p3(5:7), work 1st row patt B, p15, work 1st row patt B, p15(19:23).

2nd row K15(19:23), work 2nd row patt B, k15, work 2nd row patt B, k3(5:7), work 2nd row patt C, k3(5:7), work 2nd row patt A, k15, work 2nd row patt A, k15(19:23).

3rd row As 1st row (working 3rd patt rows).

4th row K15(19:23), work 4th row patt B, k15, work 4th row patt B, k3(5:7), work 4th row patt C, k3(5:7), work 4th row patt A, k15, work 4th row patt A, k15(19:23).

These 4 rows **form** the cable panels and **set** their position with st st panels.

Rep 1st to 3rd rows once more.

Inc row (right side) K15(19:23), work 4th row patt B, k15, work 4th row patt B, k1, m1, k2(4:6), work 4th row patt C, k2(4:6), m1, k1, work 4th row patt A, k15, work 4th row patt A, k15(19:23). 109(121:133) sts.

Taking the inc sts into st st, and working the cables on the 2nd and every foll 4th row, work 15 rows as set.

Inc row (right side) K15(19:23), work 4th row patt B, k15, work 4th row patt B, k1, m1, k3(5:7), work 4th row patt C, k3(5:7), m1, k1, work 4th row patt A, k15, work 4th row patt A, k15(19:23). 111(123:135) sts.

Taking the inc sts into st st, and working the cables on the 2nd and every foll 4th row, work 15 rows as set.

Inc row (right side) K15(19:23), work 4th row patt B, k15, work 4th row patt B, k1, m1, k4(6:8), work 4th row patt C, k4(6:8), m1, k1, work 4th row patt A, k15, work 4th row patt A, k15(19:23). 113(125:137) sts.

Taking the inc sts into st st, and working the cables on the 2nd and every foll 4th row, work 15 rows as set.

Inc row (right side) K15(19:23), work 4th row patt B, k15, work 4th row patt B, k1, m1, k5(7:9), work 4th row patt C, k5(7:9), m1, k1, work 4th row patt A, k15, work 4th row patt A, k15(19:23). 115(127:139) sts.

Taking the inc sts into st st, and working the cables on the 2nd and every foll 4th row, work 15 rows as set.
Inc row (right side) K15(19:23), work 4th row patt B, k15, work 4th row patt B, k1, m1, k6(8:10), work 4th row patt C, k6(8:10), m1, k1, work 4th row patt A, k15, work 4th row patt A, k15(19:23). 117(129:141) sts.
Cont straight until back measures approximately 29cm/ 11½in from cast on edge, ending with a 1st patt row.
Shape armholes
Cast off 7(9:11) sts at beg of next 2 rows. 103(111:119) sts.
Dec row K1, ssk, patt to last 3 sts, k2tog, k1.
Patt 1 row.
Rep the last 2 rows 5 times more. 91(99:107) sts.
Next row (right side) Patt 3(5:7), k2tog, patt 19, k2tog, patt 39(43:47), ssk, patt 19, ssk, patt 3(5:7). 87(95:103) sts.
Change to 3.75mm (US 5) needles.
Next row K35(39:43), patt 17, k35(39:43).
Rep the last row 3 times.
Next row K1, [p1, k1] 17(19:21) times, patt 17, [k1, p1] 17(19:21) times, k1.
Rep the last row until back measures 49(50:51)cm/ 19¼(19¾:20)in from cast on edge, ending with a wrong side row.
Shape shoulders
Cast off 8(9:10) sts at beg of next 4 rows and 6(7:8) sts at beg of foll 2 rows.
Leave rem 43(45:47) sts on a holder for collar.

Pocket Flaps (make 2)

With 3.75mm (US 5) needles, cast on 13 sts.
1st and 2nd rows K1, [p1, k1] to end.
3rd row K1, p1, m1, k to last 2 sts, m1, p1, k1. 15 sts.
4th row K1, p13, k1.
5th (buttonhole) row K1, p1, k4, k2tog, yf, k5, p1, k1.
6th row As 4th row.
7th row As 3rd row. 17 sts.
8th row K1, p15, k1.
9th row K1, p1, k to last 2 sts, p1, k1.
10th and 11th rows As 8th and 9th rows.

12th row As 8th row.
Leave sts on a holder.

Left Front

** With 3.75mm (US 5) needles, cast on 53(59:65) sts.
Moss st row K1, [p1, k1] to end.
Rep this row 7 times more **.
Inc row (right side) K15(19:23), p1, k2, m1, k1, p1, k15, p1, k2, m1, k1, p1, k3(5:7), p1, k2, m1, k1, [p1, k1] 3 times. 56(62:68) sts.
Change to 4mm (US 6) needles.
1st row (wrong side) K1, [p1, k1] twice, 1st row patt A, p3(5:7), 1st row patt A, p15, 1st row patt A, p15(19:23).
2nd row K15(19:23), 2nd row patt A, k15, 2nd row patt A, k3(5:7), 2nd row patt A, k1, [p1, k1] twice.
3rd row As 1st row (working 3rd row patt panel).
4th row K15(19:23), 4th row patt A, k15, 4th row patt A, k3(5:7), 4th row patt A, k1, [p1, k1] twice.
These 4 rows **form** the cable panels and **set** their position with st st panels and moss st front band.
Rep 1st to 3rd rows once more.
Inc row (right side) K15(19:23), p1, k4, p1, k15, p1, k4, p1, k1, m1, k2(4:6), p1, k4, p1, [k1, p1] twice, k1. 57(63:69) sts.
Taking the inc sts into st st, and working the cables on the 2nd and every foll 4th row, work 15 rows as set.
Inc row (right side) K15(19:23), work 4th row of patt A, k15, work 4th row of patt A, k1, m1, k3(5:7), work 4th row of patt A, [k1, p1] twice, k1. 58(64:70) sts.
Taking the inc sts into st st, and working the cables on the 2nd and every foll 4th row, work 15 rows as set.
Inc row (right side) K15(19:23), work 4th row of patt A, k15, work 4th row of patt A, k1, m1, k4(6:8), work 4th row of patt A, [k1, p1] twice, k1. 59(65:71) sts.
Taking the inc sts into st st, and working the cables on the 2nd and every foll 4th row, work 15 rows as set.
Inc row (right side) K15(19:23), work 4th row of patt A, k15, work 4th row of patt A, k1, m1, k5(7:9), work 4th row of patt A, [k1, p1] twice, k1. 60(66:72) sts.
Taking the inc sts into st st, and working the cables on the 2nd and every foll 4th row, work 15 rows as set.

Inc row (right side) K15 (19:23), work 4th row of patt A, k15, work 4th row of patt A, k1, m1, k6(8:10), work 4th row of patt A, [k1, p1] twice, k1. 61(67:73) sts.

Cont straight until front measures approximately 29cm/11½in from cast on edge, ending with a 1st patt row.

Shape armhole

Next row (right side) Cast off 7(9:11) sts, patt to end. 54(58:62) sts.

Patt 1 row.

Dec row K1, ssk, patt to end.

Patt 1 row.

Rep the last 2 rows 5 times more. 48(52:56) sts.

Next row (right side) Patt 3(5:7), k2tog, k2, p1, k5, with pocket flap sts held to front of work, [k next st of pocket flap tog with next st of front] 11 times, insert right needle into next st of flap and next 2 sts of front and k3tog, [k next st of pocket flap tog with next st of front] 5 times, patt to end. 46(50:54) sts.

Change to 3.75mm (US 5) needles.

Next row Patt 11, k35(39:43).

Next row K35(39:43), patt 11.

Next row Patt 11, k35(39:43).

Next row K1, [p1, k1] 17(19:21) times, patt 11.

Next row Patt 11, k1, [p1, k1] 17(19:21) times.

Rep the last 2 rows until 14(16:18) rows fewer have been worked than on Back to start of left shoulder shaping, so ending with a wrong side row.

Shape neck

Next row Patt to last 10 sts, k2tog, k2, [p1, k1] 3 times. 45(49:53) sts.

Keeping patt correct, cast off 9 sts at beg (neck edge) of next row, then at beg of foll wrong side rows, cast off 5 sts once, 4 sts once, 3 sts once, 2 sts once, then 1 st 0(1:2) times. 22(25:28) sts.

Patt 4 rows.

Shape shoulder

Keeping neck edge straight, cast off 8(9:10) sts at beg of next 2 right side rows.

Patt 1 row.

Cast off rem 6(7:8) sts.

Place a marker between 5th and 6th sts of 9-st centre front cast off edge for collar placement.

Place 7 button markers on moss st front band, the 1st marker on the 4th row from cast on edge, the 7th on 4th row below start of neck shaping with the rem 5 markers evenly spaced between the two.

Buttonholes will be worked on wrong side rows of Right Front moss st edge as follows:

Buttonhole row (right side) Patt to last 4 sts, p2tog, yrn, p1, k1.

Right Front

Work as Left Front from ** to **, working the 1st buttonhole on the 4th row after the cast on, following the buttonhole row instruction as given at end of the Left Front.

Change to 4mm (US 6) needles.

Inc row (right side) [K1, p1] 3 times, k2, m1, k1, p1, k3(5:7), p1, k2, m1, k1, p1, k15, p1, k2, m1, k1, p1, k15(19:23). 56(62:68) sts.

1st row (wrong side) P15(19:23), work 1st row patt B, k15, work 1st row patt B, k3(5:7), work 1st row patt B, k1, [p1, k1] twice.

This row **sets** the position of the patt panels with moss st front edge and st st panels between each cable panel and at the side edge.

Cont in patt, working buttonholes to match markers and increasing 1 st as given for left hand side of Back on the 8th row and every foll 16th row until there are 61(67:73) sts.

Cont straight until front measures approximately 29cm/ 11½in from cast on edge, ending with a 2nd patt row.

Shape armhole

Next row (wrong side) Cast off 7(9:11) sts patt to end. 54(58:62) sts.

Dec row Patt to last 3 sts, k2tog, k1.

Patt 1 row.

Rep the last 2 rows 5 times more. 48(52:56) sts.

Next row (right side) Patt 17, with pocket flap sts held to front of work, [k next st of pocket flap tog with next st of front] 5 times, insert right hand needle into next st of flap and next 2 sts of front and k3tog, [k next st of pocket flap tog with next st of front] 11 times, k5, p1, k2, ssk, patt 3(5:7). 46(50:54) sts.
Change to 3.75mm (US 5) needles.
Next row K35(39:43), patt 11.
Next row Patt 11, k35(39:43).
Next row K35(39:43), patt 11.
Next row Patt 11, k1, [p1, k1] 17(19:21) times.
Next row K1, [p1, k1] 17(19:21) times, patt 11.
Rep the last 2 rows until 14(16:18) rows fewer have been worked than on Back to right shoulder shaping, so ending with a right side row.
Shape neck
Next row Patt to last 10 sts, k2tog, k2, [p1, k1] 3 times. 45(49:53) sts.
Keeping patt correct, cast off 9 sts at beg (neck edge) of next row, then at beg of foll right side rows, cast off 5 sts once, 4 sts once, 3 sts once, 2 sts once, then 1 st 0(1:2) times. 22(25:28) sts.
Patt 4 rows.
Shape shoulder
Keeping neck edge straight, cast off 8(9:10) sts at beg of next 2 wrong side rows.
Patt 1 row.
Cast off rem 6(7:8) sts.
Place a marker between 5th and 6th sts of 9-st centre front cast off edge for collar placement.

Sleeves

With 3.75mm (US 5) needles, cast on 45(47:49) sts.
Moss st row K1, [p1, k1] to end.
Rep this row 7 times more.
Inc row (right side) K15(16:17), p1, k2, m1, k1, p1, [k1, p1] 3 times, k2, m1, k1, p1, k15(16:17). 47(49:51) sts.
Change to 4mm (US 6) needles.
1st row P15(16:17), k1, p4, k2, p1, k1, p1, k2, p4, k1, p15(16:17).

2nd row K15(16:17), p1, C4B, p1, [k1, p1] 3 times, C4F, p1, k15(16:17).
3rd row P15(16:17), k1, p4, k2, p1, k1, p1, k2, p4, k1, p15(16:17).
4th row K15(16:17), p1, k4, p1, [k1, p1] 3 times, k4, p1, k15(16:17).
These 4 rows **set** the position of the centre cable and moss st panel with st st at each side.
Patt 1 row.
Taking inc sts into st st, shape as follows:
Inc row (right side) K2, m1, patt to last 2 sts, m1, k2.
Patt 3 rows.
Rep the last 4 rows 7(8:9) times more. 63(67:71) sts.
Inc row (right side) K2, m1, patt to last 2 sts, m1, k2.
Patt 5 rows.
Rep the last 6 rows 11 times more. 87(91:95) sts.
Cont straight until sleeve measures 45(46:48)cm/ 17¾(18:19)in from cast on edge, ending with a wrong(right:wrong) side row.
Place a marker at each end of last row and patt a further 8(9:10) rows.
Shape sleeve top
Dec row K2, ssk, patt to last 4 sts, k2tog, k2.
Patt 1 row.
Rep the last 2 rows 5 times more.
Cast off rem 75(79:83) sts.

Collar

Join shoulder seams.
With right side facing, 3.75mm (US 5) needles and beg at right front marker, pick up and k28(29:30) sts up right front neck, work across 43(45:47) sts on back neck holder as follows: moss st 13(14:15), patt 17, moss st 13(14:15), pick up and k28(29:30) sts down left front neck to marker. 99(103:107) sts.
Moss st one row as set by back neck sts.
Shape back of collar
Next row (right side) Moss st 59(63:67), turn.
Next row Sl 1, moss st 18, turn.
Next row Sl 1, moss st 24, turn.

Collar

Join shoulder seams.

With right side facing, 3.75mm (US 5) needles and beg at right front marker, pick up and k28(29:30) sts up right front neck, work across 43(45:47) sts on back neck holder as follows: moss st 13(14:15), patt 17, moss st 13(14:15), pick up and k28(29:30) sts down left front neck to marker. 99(103:107) sts.

Moss st one row as set by back neck sts.

Shape back of collar

Next row (right side) Moss st 59(63:67), turn.

Next row Sl 1, moss st 18, turn.

Next row Sl 1, moss st 24, turn.

Next row Sl 1, moss st 30, turn.

Next row Sl 1, moss st 36, turn.

Next row Sl 1, moss st 42, turn.

Next row Moss st to end.

Next row Moss st across all sts.

Moss st a further 16 rows.

Cast off in moss st.

To Make Up

With centre of cast off edge of sleeve to shoulder, sew sleeves into armholes easing to fit, with row-ends above markers sewn to sts cast off at underarm and with dec rows of sleeve top matching dec rows of back and front armholes. Join side and sleeve seams. Sew on buttons.

10

Cropped Top

To fit bust	81	86	92	97	102	107	112	117	cm
	32	34	36	38	40	42	44	46	in
Finished bust	86	91	96	102	107	113	118	124	cm
	34	35¾	37¾	40	42	44½	46½	48¾	in
Length to shoulder	45	46	47	48	49	50	51	52	cm
	17¾	18	18½	19	19¼	19¾	20	20½	in

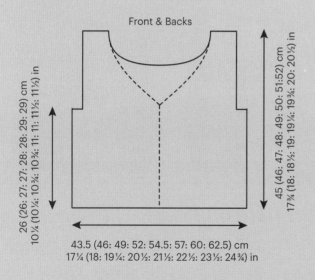

Front & Backs

26 (26: 27: 27: 28: 28: 29: 29) cm
10¼ (10¼: 10¾: 10¾: 11: 11: 11½: 11½) in

45 (46: 47: 48: 49: 50: 51:52) cm
17¾ (18: 18½: 19: 19¼: 19¾: 20: 20½) in

43.5 (46: 49: 52: 54.5: 57: 60: 62.5) cm
17¼ (18: 19¼: 20½: 21½: 22½: 23½: 24¾) in

Materials

- 3(3:3:4:4:4:5:5) 100g balls of Debbie Bliss Cotton Denim DK in New Denim 02.
- Pair each 3.25mm (US 3) and 4mm (US 6) knitting needles.
- 25cm/10in open ended zip.
- One hook and eye fastening.

Tension

22 sts and 28 rows to 10cm/4in square over st st using 4mm (US 6) needles.

Abbreviations

See page 5.

Front

With 3.25mm (US 3) needles, cast on
96(102:108:114:120:126:132:138) sts.
K 3 rows.
Change to 4mm (US 6) needles.
Beg with a k row, work in st st until front measures
26(26:27:27:28:28:29:29)cm/10¼(10¼:10¾:10¾:11:11:
11½:11½)in from cast on edge, ending with a p row.
Shape armholes
Cast off 6(6:6:7:7:7:8:8) sts at beg of next 2 rows.
84(90:96:100:106:112:116:122) sts.
Cont straight until front measures
36(37:38:39:40:41:42:43)cm/14¼(14½:15:15¼:15¾:
16¼:16½:17)in from cast on edge, ending with a p row.
Shape front neck
Next row K25(27:29:30:32:34:35:37), turn, and work
on these sts only for first side of neck, leave rem sts
on a holder.
Next row P to end.
Next row K to last 2 sts, k2tog.
Rep the last 2 rows 10 times more.
14(16:18:19:21:23:24:26) sts.
Work 1 row.
Shape shoulder
Next row Cast off 7(8:9:9:10:11:12:13) sts, k to end.
Work 1 row.
Cast off rem 7(8:9:10:11:12:12:13) sts.
With right side facing, slip centre
34(36:38:40:42:44:46:48) sts onto a holder, rejoin
yarn to rem sts, k to end.
Next row P to end.
Next row Skpo, k to end.
Rep the last 2 rows 10 times more.
14(16:18:19:21:23:24:26) sts.
Work 2 rows.
Shape shoulder
Next row Cast off 7(8:9:9:10:11:12:13) sts, p to end.
Work 1 row.
Cast off rem 7(8:9:10:11:12:12:13) sts.

Right Back

With 3.25mm (US 3) needles, cast on
48(51:54:57:60:63:66:69) sts.
K 3 rows.
Change to 4mm (US 6) needles.
1st row K to end.
2nd row K3, p to end.
These 2 rows **form** the st st with garter st edging
and are repeated.
Work straight until back measures
26(26:27:27:28:28:29:29)cm/10¼(10¼:10¾:10¾:11:11:
11½:11½)in from cast on edge, ending with a wrong
side row.
Shape armhole
Next row Cast off 6(6:6:7:7:7:8:8) sts, k to last 3 sts,
place these 3 sts on a holder.
39(42:45:47:50:53:55:58) sts.
Next row P to end.
Shape back neck
1st row K to last 2 sts, skpo.
2nd row P to end.
Rep the last 2 rows 24(25:26:27:28:29:30:31) times.
14(16:18:19:21:23:24:26) sts.
Work straight until back measures the same as Front
to shoulder shaping, ending at armhole edge.
Shape shoulder
Next row Cast off 7(8:9:9:10:11:12:13) sts, k to end.
Work 1 row.
Cast off rem 7(8:9:10:11:12:12:13) sts.

Left Back

With 3.25mm (US 3) needles, cast on
48(51:54:57:60:63:66:69) sts.
K 3 rows.
Change to 4mm (US 6) needles.
1st row K to end.
2nd row P to last 3 sts, k3.
These 2 rows **form** the st st with garter st edging
and are repeated.

Work straight until back measures 26(26:27:27:28:28:29:29)cm/10¼(10¼:10¾:10¾:11:11:11½:11½)in from cast in edge, ending with a wrong side row.

Shape armhole

Next row K3, slip these 3 sts onto a holder, k to end.

Next row Cast off 6(6:6:7:7:7:8:8) sts, p to end. 39(42:45:47:50:53:55:58) sts.

Shape back neck

1st row K2tog, k to end.

2nd row P to end.

Rep the last 2 rows 24(25:26:27:28:29:30:31) times. 14(16:18:19:21:23:24:26) sts.

Work straight until back measures the same as Front to shoulder shaping, ending at armhole edge.

Shape shoulder

Next row Cast off 7(8:9:9:10:11:12:13) sts, k to end.

Work 1 row.

Cast off rem 7(8:9:10:11:12:12:13) sts.

Neckband

Join shoulder seams.

With right side facing and 3.25mm (US 3) needles, slip 3 sts from left back onto a needle, pick up and k38(40:40:42:42:44:44:46) sts up left back neck, 17 sts down left front neck, k34(36:38:40:42:44:46:48) sts from front neck holder, pick up and k17 sts up right front neck, then 38(40:40:42:42:44:44:46) sts down right back neck, k3 from holder. 150(156:158:164:166:172:174:180) sts.

1st row Skpo, k to last 2 sts, k2tog.

2nd row K to end.

Rep the last 2 rows once more.

Cast off, decreasing on this row as before.

Armbands

With right side facing and 3.25mm (US 3) needles, pick up and k7(7:7:8:8:8:9:9) sts across armhole cast off sts, 76(80:80:84:84:88:88:92) sts along row-ends, then pick up and k7(7:7:8:8:8:9:9) sts across cast off armhole sts. 90(94:94:100:100:104:106:110) sts.

1st row K5(5:5:6:6:6:7:7), k2tog, skpo, k to last 9(9:9:10:10:10:11:11) sts, k2tog, skpo, k5(5:5:6:6:6:7:7).

2nd row K to end.

3rd row K4(4:4:5:5:5:6:6), k2tog, skpo, k to last 8(8:8:9:9:9:10:10) sts, k2tog, skpo, k4(4:4:5:5:5:6:6).

4th row K to end.

Cast off, decreasing on this row as before.

To Make Up

Join side seams. With top of zip level with start of neck shaping and leaving 2(2:3:3:4:4:5:5)cm/¾(¾:1¼:1¼:1½:1½:2:2)in free at bottom, sew in zip.

11

Denim Lace-Back Top

To fit bust	81 – 86	92 – 97	102 – 107	cm
	32 – 34	36 – 38	40 – 42	in
Finished bust	43	49	54	cm
	17	19¼	21¼	in
Length to shoulder	50	53	56	cm
	19¾	20¾	22	in

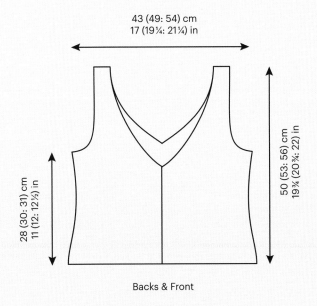

43 (49: 54) cm
17 (19¼: 21¼) in

50 (53: 56) cm
19¾ (20¾: 22) in

28 (30: 31) cm
11 (12: 12½) in

Backs & Front

Materials

- 3(3:4) 100g balls of Debbie Bliss Cotton Denim DK in Mid Blue 04.
- Pair of 3.75mm (US 5) knitting needles.
- 14 x 4mm silver eyelets, with eyelet pliers or a fixing tool and hammer.
- 1mt/1yd of ribbon/cord/tape or similar.

Tension

23 sts and 31 rows to 10cm/4in square over st st using 3.75mm (US 5) needles.

Abbreviations

See page 5.

Front

With 3.75mm (US 5) needles, cast on 101(115:127) sts.
K 1 row.
Beg with a k row, work in st st.
Work 8 rows.
Dec row K30(32:34), ssk, k37(47:55), k2tog, k30(32:34).

Work 5 rows.

Rep the last 6 rows 4 times more then the dec row again. 89(103:115) sts.

Work 9 rows.

Inc row K30(32:34), m1, k to last 30(32:34) sts, m1, k to end.

Work 7 rows.

Rep the last 8 rows 3 times more, then the inc row once more. 99(113:125) sts.

Work 5(11:19) rows without shaping, so ending with a p row.

Shape armholes and front neck

Next row (right side) Cast off 7(8:9) sts purlwise, with one st on needle after cast off, k next 41(47:52) sts, p1, k to end.

Next row Cast off 7(8:9) sts knitwise, with one st on needle after cast off, p next 40(46:51) sts, k1, p1, k1, p to end. 85(97:107) sts.

Next row (right side) P1, k1, p1, ssk, k35(41:46) sts, p1, [k1, p1] twice, k to last 5 sts, k2tog, p1, k1, p1.

Next row K1, p1, k1, p36(42:47) sts, k1, [p1, k1] twice, p to last 3 sts, k1, p1, k1. 83(95:105) sts.

Divide for neck

Next row (right side) P1, k1, p1, ssk, k32(38:43) sts, k2tog, p1, k1, p1, turn and cont on these 40(46:51) sts only, leave rem sts on a spare needle.

**** Next row** K1, p1, k1, p to last 3 sts, k1, p1, k1.

Next row P1, k1, p1, ssk, k to last 5 sts, k2tog, p1, k1, p1.

Rep the last 2 rows 5(6:7) times more. 28(32:35) sts.

Keeping 3 sts at each edge in rib as set and armhole edge straight, cont to dec at neck edge only on every foll right side row, until 11 sts rem.

Cont straight in patt until front measures 50(53:56)cm/ 19¾(20¾:22)in from cast on edge.

Cast off **.

With right side facing, rejoin yarn to 41(47:52) sts on spare needle, p1, k1, p1, k to last 5 sts, k2tog, p1, k1, p1. Now work as first side of neck from ** to **.

Right Back

With 3.75mm (US 5) needles, cast on 49(56:61) sts. K 2 rows.

Next row (wrong side) Cast on 5 sts, k1, p to end. 54(61:66) sts.

1st patt row K to end.

2nd patt row K1, p3, sl 1, pull yarn tight, p to end. Rep the last 2 rows twice more.

Dec row (right side) K6, ssk, k to end.

Next row As 2nd patt row.

Next row As 1st patt row.

Next row As 2nd patt row.

Eyelet row (right side) K to last 3 sts, yf, k2tog, k1.

Next row As 2nd patt row.

Dec row (right side) K6, ssk, k to end.

Cont in this way to work side decs on 4 foll 6th rows, **at the same time**, rep the eyelet row with 11 patt rows between each eyelet. 48(55:60) sts.

After last side dec row, patt 9 rows, then work side inc rows as follows:

Inc row (right side) K6, m1, patt to end.

Patt 7 rows (working eyelet row on 2nd row).

Cont to work 4 more eyelet rows (7 eyelets in total) and inc rows on next row and 3 foll 8th rows. 53(60:65) sts.

Patt 2 rows after 7th eyelet row, so ending with a right side row.

Shape neck

Next row Cast off 5 sts knitwise, p to end.

Next row K to last 5 sts, k2tog, p1, k1, p1.

Next row K1, p1, k1, p to end.

Work 0(6:14) rows more as set, ending with a wrong side row. 47(51:52) sts.

Shape armhole and neck

Next row (right side) Cast off 7 sts purlwise, k to last 5 sts, k2tog, p1, k1, p1.

Next row K1, p1, k1, p to last 3 sts, k1, p1, k1.

Next row P1, k1, p1, ssk, k to last 5 sts, k2tog, p1, k1, p1.

Rep the last 2 rows 6(7:8) times more.

Keeping 3 sts in rib at each end and armhole edge straight, cont to dec at neck edge only on every right side row as set until 11 sts rem.

Work straight until back matches Front to shoulder. Cast off.

Left Back

With 3.75mm (US 5) needles, cast on 49(56:61) sts.
K 1 row.
Next row (right side) Cast on 5 sts, k to end. 54(61:66) sts.
1st patt row P to last 5 sts, sl 1, pull yarn tight, p3, k1.
2nd patt row K to end.
Rep the last 2 rows twice more, then 1st patt row again.
Dec row (right side) K to last 8 sts, k2tog, k6.
Next row As 1st patt row.
Next row As 2nd patt row.
Next row As 1st patt row.
Eyelet row (right side) K1, k2tog, yf, k to end.
Next row As 1st patt row.
Dec row (right side) K to last 8 sts, k2tog, k6.
Cont in this way to work side decs on 4 foll 6th rows, **at the same time**, rep the eyelet row with 11 patt rows between each eyelet. 48(55:60) sts.
After last side dec row, patt 9 rows, then work side inc rows as follows:
Inc row (right side) K to last 6 sts, m1, k6.
Patt 7 rows (working eyelet row on 2nd row).
Cont to work 4 more eyelet rows (7 eyelets in total) and inc rows on next row and 3 foll 8th rows. 53(60:65) sts.
Patt 1 row after 7th eyelet row, so ending with a wrong side row.
Shape neck
Next row (right side) Cast off 5 sts purlwise, k to end.
Next row P to last 3 sts, k1, p1, p1.
Next row P1, k1, p1, ssk, k to end.
Work 0(6:14) rows more as set, ending with a right side row. 47(51:52) sts.
Shape armhole and neck
Next row Cast off 7 sts knitwise, p to last 3 sts, k1, p1, k1.
Next row P1, k1, p1, ssk, k to last 5 sts, k2tog, p1, k1, p1.
Next row K1, p1, k1, p to last 3 sts, k1, p1, k1.
Rep the last 2 rows 6(7:8) times more.

Keeping 3 sts in rib at each end and armhole edge straight, cont to dec at neck edge on every right side row as set until 11 sts rem.
Work straight until back matches Front to shoulder. Cast off.

To Make Up

Join shoulder seams.
Fold back facings onto the wrong side, and slip stitch in place. Line up the eyelet holes of the facing with the 3rd stitch of the right side of the front and put each eyelet through the centre of this stitch and the eyelet hole, then fix the eyelets in place securely. Join the side seams. Thread the ribbon or similar through the eyelets, lacing from side to side.

12

Cricket Sweater

To fit bust	81 – 86	92 – 97	102 – 107	112 – 117	cm
	32 – 34	36 – 38	40 – 42	44 – 46	in
Finished bust	108	118	131	141	cm
	42½	46½	51¾	55½	in
Length to shoulder	62	64	66	68	cm
	24½	25¼	26	26¾	in

Sleeve Length 48cm/19in for all sizes

Materials

- 7(7:8:8) 100g balls Debbie Bliss Cotton Denim DK in Pale Blue 05 (M) and one 50g ball in each of Rose 10 (A) and Milk 06 (B).
- Pair each size 3.75mm (US 5) and 4mm (US 6) knitting needles.
- 3.75mm (US 5) and 4mm (US 6) circular needles for larger sizes.
- Cable needle.

Tension

26 sts and 32 rows to 10cm/4in square over patt, using 4mm (US 6) needles.

Abbreviations

C4F = slip next 2 sts onto cable needle and leave at front of work, k2, then k2 from cable needle. Also see page 5.

Back

With 3.75mm (US 5) needles and M, cast on 128(141:155:168) sts.
1st and 3rd sizes only
1st rib row P2, [p2, k3, p2, k2] to last 9 sts, p2, k3, p4.
2nd rib row P2, [k2, p3, k2, p2] to end.
2nd and 4th sizes only
1st rib row K4, [p2, k3, p2, k2] to last 2 sts, k2.
2nd rib row K2, p2, [k2, p3, k2, p2] to last 2 sts, k2.
All sizes
These 2 rows **form** the rib with garter st edging.
Rep the last 2 rows for 11cm/4¼in, ending with a 1st rib row.
Inc row Rib 2(4:2:4), [k2, p1, m1 purlwise, p2, k2, p2] to last 0(2:0:2) sts, k0(2:0:2). 142(156:172:186) sts.
Change to 4mm (US 6) needles and work in patt as follows:
1st row (right side) P0(2:0:2), k2, [p2, k4, p2, k2] to last 0(2:0:2) sts, p0(2:0:2).
2nd row K0(2:0:2), p2, [k2, p4, k2, p2] to last 0(2:0:2) sts, k0(2:0:2).

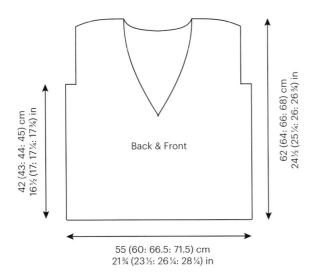

Back & Front

42 (43: 44: 45) cm
16½ (17: 17¼: 17¾) in

62 (64: 66: 68) cm
24½ (25¼: 26: 26¾) in

55 (60: 66.5: 71.5) cm
21¾ (23½: 26¼: 28¼) in

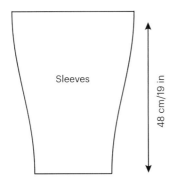

Sleeves

48 cm/19 in

3rd row P0(2:0:2), k2, [p2, C4F, p2, k2] to last 0(2:0:2) sts, p0(2:0:2).

4th row K0(2:0:2), p2, [k2, p4, k2, p2] to last 0(2:0:2) sts, k0(2:0:2).

These 4 rows **form** the patt and are repeated throughout.

Cont in patt until back measures 42(43:44:45)cm/ 16½(17:17¼:17¾)in from cast on edge, ending with a wrong side row.

Shape armholes

Cast off 8(10:12:14) sts at beg of next 2 rows. 126(136:148:158) sts.

Cont straight until back measures 58(60:62:64)cm/ 22¾(23½:24½:25¼)in from cast on edge, ending with a wrong side row.

Shape neck

Next row Patt 31(34:37:41) sts, turn and work on these sts only for first side of neck shaping.

Dec one st at neck edge on the next 4 wrong side rows. 27(30:33:37) sts.

Shape upper arm

Cast off 5(6:6:7) sts at beg of next row and 2 foll right side rows. 12(12:15:16) sts.

Work 1 row.

Shape shoulder

Cast off rem 12(12:15:16) sts.

With right side facing, rejoin yarn to rem sts, patt 5(2:5:1), * [k2tog] twice, patt 6; rep from * 4(5:5:6) times more, [k2tog] twice, patt 5(2:5:1), leave these 52(54:60:60) sts on a holder, patt to end.

Dec one st at neck edge on the next 4 wrong side rows. 27(30:33:37) sts.

Work 1 row.

Shape upper arm

Cast off 5(6:6:7) sts at beg of next row and 2 foll wrong side rows. 12(12:15:16) sts.

Work 1 row.

Shape shoulder

Cast off rem 12(12:15:16) sts.

Front

Work as given for Back until 32 rows fewer have been worked than on Back to armhole shaping, ending with a wrong side row.

Shape neck

Next row Patt 68(75:83:90) sts, work 2tog, turn and work on these 69(76:84:91) sts for first side of neck. Work 1 row.

Dec one st at neck edge on next row and 14 foll right side rows. 54(61:69:76) sts.
Work 1 row.

Shape armhole

Next row Cast off 8(10:12:14) sts, patt to last 2 sts, work 2tog. 45(50:56:61) sts.
Patt 1 row.
Keeping armhole edge straight, cont to dec 1 st at neck edge on every foll right side row until 27(30:33:37) sts rem.
Cont straight until front matches Back to upper arm shaping, ending at armhole edge.

Shape upper arm

Cast off 5(6:6:7) sts at beg of next row and 2 foll right side rows. 12(12:15:16) sts.
Work 1 row.

Shape shoulder

Cast off rem 12(12:15:16) sts.
With right side facing, slip centre 2 sts onto a holder, rejoin yarn to rem sts, work 2 tog, patt to end.
Work 1 row.
Dec one st at neck edge on next row and 15 foll right side rows. 54(61:69:76) sts.

Shape armhole

Next row Cast off 8(10:12:14) sts, patt to end. 45(50:56:61) sts.
Keeping armhole edge straight, cont to dec at neck edge on every foll right side row until 27(30:33:37) sts rem.
Cont straight until front matches Back to shoulder shaping, ending at armhole edge.

Shape upper arm

Cast off 5(6:6:7) sts at beg of next row and 2 foll wrong side rows. 12(12:15:16) sts.
Work 1 row.

Shape shoulder

Cast off rem 12(12:15:16) sts.

Sleeves

With 3.75mm (US 5) needles and M, cast on 56(56:65:65) sts.
1st rib row K2, [p2, k3, p2, k2] to end.

2nd rib row P2, [k2, p3, k2, p2] to end.
These 2 rows **form** the rib.
Rep the last 2 rows for 11cm/4¼in, ending with a 1st rib row.
Inc row P2, [k2, p1, m1 purlwise, p2, k2, p2] to end. 62(62:72:72) sts.
Change to 4mm (US 6) needles and work in patt as follows:
1st row (right side) K2, [p2, k4, p2, k2] to end.
2nd row P2, [k2, p4, k2, p2] to end.
3rd row K2, [p2, C4F, p2, k2] to end.
4th row P2, [k2, p4, k2, p2] to end.
These 4 rows **form** the patt.
Keeping patt correct and working in stripes of 4 rows A, 2 rows B, 4 rows A, 2 rows M, 4 rows B, 2 rows A, 4 rows B, 2 rows M, 4 rows A, 2 rows B, 4 rows A, then cont in M only, **at the same time,** inc one st at each end of the next row and 6 foll 6th rows. 76(76:86:86) sts.
Now inc on every foll 4th row until there are 104(108:114:118) sts, working all inc sts into patt.
Cont straight until sleeve measures 48cm/19in from cast on edge, ending with a wrong side row.
Place a marker at each end of last row.
Work a further 10(12:16:18) rows.
Cast off in patt.

Neckband

Join shoulder seams.
With right side facing and 3.75mm (US 5) circular needle and B, pick up and k76(80:84:88) sts down left front neck, k2 from safety pin, pick up and k76(80:84:88) sts up right front neck, 13(12:13:13) sts down right back neck, rib across 52(54:60:60) sts from back neck holder, then pick up and k13(12:13:13) sts up left back neck. 232(240:256:264) sts.
Cont to work in rounds as follows:
Next round [K2, p2] to end.
Next round K2, [p2, k2] 18(19:20:21) times, p1, k2tog, skpo, p1, [k2, p2] to end.
Next round K2, [p2, k2] 18(19:20:21) times, k2tog, skpo, [k2, p2] to end.

Work a further 19 rounds in stripes of 1 round B, 2 rounds A, 4 rounds B, 10 rounds M, decreasing 2 sts on every round.
Cast off in rib, decreasing 2 sts at centre front on this round as before.

To Make Up

Sew sleeves into armholes, with row-ends above markers to cast off sts at beg of armhole shaping. Join sleeve and side seam to top of welt.

13

Wrapover Waistcoat

To fit bust	86	92	97	102	cm
	34	36	38	40	in
Finished bust	96	102	107	112	cm
	38	40	42	44	in
Length to shoulder	50	52	54	57	cm
	19¾	20½	21¼	22½	in

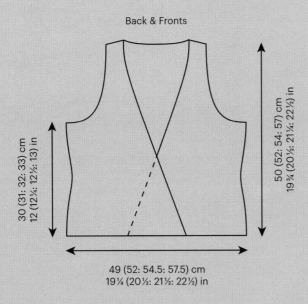

Back & Fronts

30 (31: 32: 33) cm
12 (12¼: 12½: 13) in

49 (52: 54.5: 57.5) cm
19¼ (20½: 21½: 22½) in

50 (52: 54: 57) cm
19¾ (20½: 21¼: 22½) in

Materials

- 3(4:4:5) 100g balls of Debbie Bliss Cotton Denim DK in New Denim 02.
- Pair each 3.25mm (US 3) and 3.75mm (US 5) knitting needles.
- 1m/1⅛yds of 3cm/1¼in wide suede strip or ribbon for ties.

Tension

22 sts and 30 rows to 10cm/4in square over st st using 3.75mm (US 5) needles.

Abbreviations

See page 5.

Back

With 3.25mm (US 3) needles, cast on 108(114:120:126) sts.
K 1 row.
Change to 3.75mm (US 5) needles.
Beg with a k row, work in st st.
Work 6 rows.

Dec row K7, skpo, k to last 9 sts, k2tog, k7.
Work 3 rows.
Rep the last 4 rows 4 times more then the dec row
again. 96(102:108:114) sts.
Work 13(15:17:19) rows.
Inc row K7, m1, k to last 7 sts, m1, k7.
Work 5 rows.
Rep the last 6 rows 4 times more then the inc row
again. 108(114:120:126) sts.
Cont straight until back measures 30(31:32:33)cm/
12(12¼:12½:13)in from cast on edge, ending with a p row.
Shape armholes
Cast off 9(9:10:10) sts at beg of next 2 rows.
90(96:100:106) sts.
2nd, 3rd and 4th sizes only
Next row K2, skpo, k to last 4 sts, k2tog, k2.
Next row K3, p to last 3 sts, k3.
Rep the last 2 rows –(2:4:6) times more.
All sizes
Next row K to end.
Next row K3, p to last 3 sts, k3.
Next row K2, skpo, k to last 4 sts, k2tog, k2.
Next row K3, p to last 3 sts, k3. 88(88:88:90) sts.
Rep the last 4 rows until 60(62:62:64) sts rem,
ending with a wrong side row.
Shape shoulders
Cast off 10 sts at beg of next 2 rows.
Cast off rem 40(42:42:44) sts.

Left Front

With 3.25mm (US 3) needles, cast on 68(71:75:78) sts.
K 1 row.
Change to 3.75mm (US 5) needles.
Next row K to end.
Next row K3, p to end.
These 2 rows **form** st st with garter st front border.
Rep the last 2 rows twice more.
Shape side and front neck
Dec row K7, skpo, k to last 6 sts, k2tog, k4.
Next row K3, p to end.

Next row K to end.
Next row K3, p to end.
Rep the last 4 rows 4 times more and the dec row
again. 56(59:63:66) sts.
Keeping side edge straight, cont to dec at front edge
on every foll 4th row and work 13(15:17:19) rows.
53(56:59:62) sts.
Cont to shape front edge on every foll 4th row.
Inc row K7, m1, work to end.
Work 5 rows.
Rep the last 6 rows 4 times more and the inc row again.
Keeping side edge straight, cont to dec at front edge
on every 4th row until side seam measures same as
Back to armhole shaping, ending with a wrong side row.
Shape armhole
Cont to dec at front edge throughout as set.
Cast off 9(9:10:10) sts at beg of the next row.
Next row K3, p to last 3 sts, k3.
2nd, 3rd and 4th sizes only
Next row K2, skpo, work to end.
Next row K3, p to last 3 sts, k3.
Rep the last 2 rows –(2:4:6) times more.
All sizes
Next row (right side) Work to end.
Next row K3, p to last 3 sts, k3.
Next row K2, skpo, work to end.
Next row K3, p to last 3 sts, k3.
Rep the last 4 rows 4(3:2:2) times more.
Next row Work to last 3 sts, slip these 3 sts onto
a safety pin.
Cont to dec at front edge until a total of 31(32:33:34)
sts of front have been decreased, then keep neck edge
straight, **at the same time,** cont to dec at armhole
edge on every 4th row until 10 sts rem, ending with
a wrong side row.
Shape shoulder
Cast off.

Right Front

With 3.25mm (US 3) needles, cast on 68(71:75:78) sts.
K 1 row.
Change to 3.75mm (US 5) needles.
Next row K to end.
Next row P to last 3 sts, k3.
These 2 rows **form** st st with garter st front border.
Rep the last 2 rows twice more.
Shape side and front neck
Dec row K4, skpo, k to last 9 sts, k2tog, k7.
Next row P to last 3 sts, k3.
Next row K to end.
Next row P to last 3 sts, k3.
Rep the last 4 rows 4 times more then the dec row
again. 56(59:63:66) sts rem.
Keeping side edge straight, cont to dec at front
edge on every foll 4th row and work 13(15:17:19) rows.
53(56:59:62) sts.
Cont to dec at front edge throughout.
Inc row Work to last 7 sts, m1, k7.
Work 5 rows.
Rep the last 6 rows 4 times more then the inc row again.
Keeping side edge straight, cont to dec at front edge
on every 4th row until side seam measures same as
back to armhole shaping, ending with a right side row.
Shape armhole
Cont to dec at front edge on every 4th row.
Cast off 9(9:10:10) sts at beg of the next row.
2nd, 3rd and 4th sizes only
Next row (right side) Work to last 4 sts, k2tog, k2.
Next row K3, p to last 3 sts, k3.
Rep the last 2 rows (2:4:6) times more.
All sizes
Next row (right side) Work to end.
Next row K3, p to last 3 sts, k3.
Next row Work to last 4 sts, k2tog, k2.
Next row K3, p to last 3 sts, k3.
Rep the last 4 rows 4(3:2:2) times more.
Next row K3, slip these 3 sts onto a safety pin,
work to end.

Cont to dec at front edge until a total of 31(32:33:34)
sts of front have been decreased, then keep neck edge
straight, **at the same time,** cont to dec at armhole
edge until 10 sts rem, ending with a right side row.
Shape shoulder
Cast off.

Collar

Join shoulder seams.
With 3.25mm (US 3) needles, slip 3 sts from right front
safety pin onto a needle, pick up and k40(40:42:42) sts
up right front neck to shoulder, 50(50:54:54) sts from
back neck, 40(40:42:42) sts down left front neck, then
k3 from front neck safety pin. 136(136:144:144) sts.
Next row K5, [p2, k2] to last 7 sts, p2, k5.
This row **sets** the k2, p2 rib with k3 garter st border.
Next 2 rows Rib to last 47 sts, turn.
Next 2 rows Rib to last 39 sts, turn.
Next 2 rows Rib to last 31 sts, turn.
Next 2 rows Rib to last 23 sts, turn.
Next 2 rows Rib to last 15 sts, turn.
Next 2 rows Rib to last 7 sts, turn.
Next row Rib to last 3 sts, k3.
Cont in rib with garter st border across all sts for
a further 8cm/3¼in.
Cast off in rib.

To Make Up

Cut the suede strip or ribbon in half and sew one piece
to the right front edge. Join the side seams, enclosing
and rem suede strip or ribbon in the left side seam.